FENCHURCH STREET TO BARKING

J.E.CONNOR
in association with
Charles Phillips

Series editor Vic Mitchell

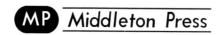

MP Middleton Press

A Fenchurch Street-Southend train, headed by rebuilt Class 37 4-4-2T No 47 *Stratford* enters Plaistow station around 1911, and passes a Metropolitan District Railway electric unit awaiting departure from the bay platform. (Locomotive Publishing Company)

First Published August 1998

ISBN 1 901706 20 6

© *Middleton Press*

Cover design Deborah Goodridge

Published by
  Middleton Press
  Easebourne Lane
  Midhurst, West Sussex
  GU29 9AZ
Tel: 01730 813169
Fax: 01730 812601

Layout and typesetting London Railway Record

Printed & bound by Biddles Ltd.
  Guildford and Kings Lynn

CONTENTS

ACKNOWLEDGEMENTS

I should like to thank the various photographers, without whom this volume would not have been possible, together with Charles Phillips for help received. I am also grateful to Dr. Edwin Course who kindly read the proofs, and made a number of very helpful comments.

Lastly, but by no means least, thanks must go to my son Charlie for producing the maps, and to Tricia and Barbie for their general assistance.

GEOGRAPHICAL SETTING

The entire route is on the northern flank of the lower Thames Valley. It crosses two tributaries of the River Thames; the River Lea, near Bromley, and the River Roding, where it joins Barking Creek at Barking.

The boundary between London and Metropolitan Essex was just east of Bromley until the formation of the Greater London boroughs from 1st April 1965, when the Essex boundary was moved to a point east of Upminster. This change reflected the steady urbanisation of the almost flat area.

The maps are at exactly 15ins to 1 mile, and they have north at the top.

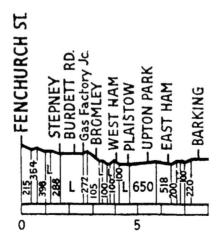

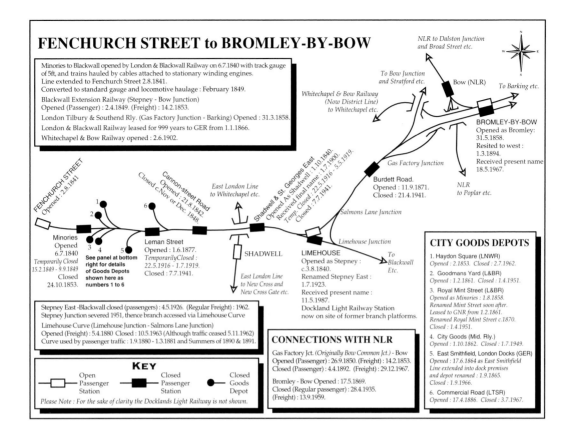

FENCHURCH STREET to BROMLEY-BY-BOW

Minories to Blackwall opened by London & Blackwall Railway on 6.7.1840 with track gauge of 5ft, and trains hauled by cables attached to stationary winding engines.
Line extended to Fenchurch Street. 2.8.1841.
Converted to standard gauge and locomotive haulage : February 1849.
Blackwall Extension Railway (Stepney - Bow Junction)
Opened (Passenger) : 2.4.1849. (Freight) : 14.2.1853.
London Tilbury & Southend Rly. (Gas Factory Junction - Barking) Opened : 31.3.1858.
London & Blackwall Railway leased for 999 years to GER from 1.1.1866.
Whitechapel & Bow Railway opened : 2.6.1902.

NLR to Dalston Junction
and Broad Street etc.

To Bow Junction
and Stratford etc.

Bow (NLR)

To Barking etc.

Whitechapel & Bow Railway
(Now District Line)
to Whitechapel etc.

BROMLEY-BY-BOW
Opened as Bromley:
31.5.1858.
Resited to west :
1.3.1894.
Received present name
18.5.1967.

FENCHURCH STREET
Opened : 2.8.1841

Cannon-street Road
Opened : 21.8.1842
Closed c.Nov or Dec. 1848.

East London Line
to Whitechapel etc.

Shadwell & St. Georges East
Opened As Shadwell : 1.10.1840.
Received final name : 1.7.1900.
Temp. Closed : 22.5.1916 - 5.5.1919.
Closed : 7.7.1941.

Gas Factory Junction

Burdett Road.
Opened : 11.9.1871.
Closed : 21.4.1941.

NLR
to Poplar etc.

Salmons Lane Junction

Minories
Opened
6.7.1840
Temporarily Closed
15.2.1849 - 9.9.1849
Closed
24.10.1853.

Leman Street
Opened : 1.6.1877.
Temporarily Closed :
22.5.1916 - 1.7.1919.
Closed : 7.7.1941.

SHADWELL

LIMEHOUSE
Opened as Stepney :
c.3.8.1840.
Renamed Stepney East :
1.7.1923.
Received present name :
11.5.1987.
Dockland Light Railway Station
now on site of former branch platforms.

Limehouse Junction

To
Blackwall
Etc.

See panel at bottom
right for details
of Goods Depots
shown here as
numbers 1 to 6

East London Line
to New Cross and
New Cross Gate etc.

CITY GOODS DEPOTS

1. Haydon Square (LNWR)
Opened : 2.1.1853. Closed : 2.7.1962.
2. Goodmans Yard (L&BR)
Opened : 1.2.1861. Closed : 1.4.1951.
3. Royal Mint Street (L&BR)
Opened as Minories : 1.8.1858.
Renamed Mint Street soon after.
Leased to GNR from 1.2.1861.
Renamed Royal Mint Street c.1870.
Closed : 1.4.1951.
4. City Goods (Mid. Rly.)
Opened : 1.10.1862. Closed : 1.7.1949.
5. East Smithfield, London Docks (GER)
Opened : 17.6.1864 as East Smithfield
Line extended into dock premises
and depot renamed : 1.9.1865.
Closed : 1.9.1966.
6. Commercial Road (LTSR)
Opened : 17.4.1886. Closed : 3.7.1967.

Stepney East -Blackwall closed (passengers) : 4.5.1926. (Regular Freight) : 1962.
Stepney Junction severed 1951, thence branch accessed via Limehouse Curve
Limehouse Curve (Limehouse Junction - Salmons Lane Junction)
Opened (Freight) : 5.4.1880 Closed : 10.5.1963 (Although traffic ceased 5.11.1962)
Curve used by passenger traffic : 1.9.1880 - 1.3.1881 and Summers of 1890 & 1891.

CONNECTIONS WITH NLR

Gas Factory Jct. (Originally Bow Common Jct.) - Bow
Opened (Passenger) : 26.9.1850. (Freight) : 14.2.1853.
Closed (Passenger) : 4.4.1892. (Freight) : 29.12.1967.

Bromley-Bow Opened : 17.5.1869.
Closed (Regular passenger) : 28.4.1935.
(Freight) : 13.9.1959.

KEY

| | Open Passenger Station | | Closed Passenger Station | | Closed Goods Depot |

Please Note : For the sake of clarity the Docklands Light Railway is not shown.

HISTORICAL BACKGROUND

The line serving Fenchurch Street owes its origins to the London & Blackwall Railway which was built for cable-haulage, and had a track gauge of around 5ft. It received the Royal Assent on 28th July 1836.

The system of cable-haulage was adopted as it was thought that sparks from locomotives could set fire to wooden ships berthed in adjoining docks.

At first, the City Corporation would not allow the line to enter their exclusive square mile, so the Company reluctantly settled for a terminus at The Minories. By 1839 however, the authorities relented, and agreed to the route being extended 415 yards westwards into a station at Fenchurch Street.

Stationary winding engines were positioned at Minories and Blackwall, and the line was double throughout. However, because of the method of operation, these were used for bi-directional running, and therefore not designated as either 'up' or 'down'. The system of cable haulage was ingenious to say the least, but passengers wishing to make a journey between two intermediate stations had to travel into one of the termini first.

The line was ceremonially opened between the Minories and Blackwall on Saturday 4th July 1840, although at the time only one track was in operation. The public service started on Monday 6th July, and the second track was brought into use a month later.

At the start of a working day, there would be trains at either terminus, gripped to the rope, and coaches at each intermediate station. Following a telegraphic signal from one end to the other, the winding engines would be set in motion, and begin hauling the carriages towards them. Each vehicle was manned by a guard, and when trains approached the first station, the last coach

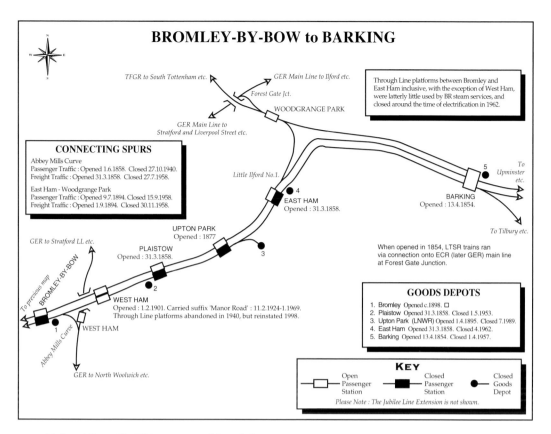

BROMLEY-BY-BOW to BARKING

TFGR to South Tottenham etc.

GER Main Line to Ilford etc.

Forest Gate Jct.

WOODGRANGE PARK

Through Line platforms between Bromley and East Ham inclusive, with the exception of West Ham, were latterly little used by BR steam services, and closed around the time of electrification in 1962.

GER Main Line to Stratford and Liverpool Street etc.

CONNECTING SPURS

Abbey Mills Curve
Passenger Traffic : Opened 1.6.1858. Closed 27.10.1940.
Freight Traffic : Opened 31.3.1858. Closed 27.7.1958.

East Ham - Woodgrange Park
Passenger Traffic : Opened 9.7.1894. Closed 15.9.1958.
Freight Traffic : Opened 1.9.1894. Closed 30.11.1958.

Little Ilford No.1.

5 — To Upminster etc.

4
EAST HAM
Opened : 31.3.1858.

BARKING
Opened : 13.4.1854.

UPTON PARK
Opened : 1877

GER to Stratford LL etc.

PLAISTOW
Opened : 31.3.1858.

3

To Tilbury etc.

When opened in 1854, LTSR trains ran via connection onto ECR (later GER) main line at Forest Gate Junction.

BROMLEY-BY-BOW

To previous map

2

GOODS DEPOTS

1. Bromley Opened c.1898. ☐
2. Plaistow Opened 31.3.1858. Closed 1.5.1953.
3. Upton Park (LNWR) Opened 1.4.1895. Closed 7.1989.
4. East Ham Opened 31.3.1858. Closed 4.1962.
5. Barking Opened 13.4.1854. Closed 1.4.1957.

WEST HAM
Opened : 1.2.1901. Carried suffix 'Manor Road' : 11.2.1924-1.1969.
Through Line platforms abandoned in 1940, but reinstated 1998.

1

WEST HAM

Abbey Mills Curve

GER to North Woolwich etc.

KEY

| ▭ Open Passenger Station | ◼ Closed Passenger Station | ● Closed Goods Depot |

Please Note : The Jubilee Line Extension is not shown.

---

would be 'slipped'. This was achieved by removal of a pin from the coupling, and releasing its gripper from the rope. Once detached from the other vehicles, it would then freewheel towards the platform, and be stopped by means of a handbrake applied by the guard.

The system was fine when all was working well, but it seems that there were numerous problems with cables twisting or breaking. For all its shortcomings however, the London & Blackwall was a decidedly innovative undertaking, and can probably claim to be the world's first rapid transit system. Its day to day running relied partly on the Cooke & Wheatstone electric telegraph, and although this was used on other lines, the LBR is thought to be the first railway to employ it throughout its entire length.

All passengers paid a flat fare, regardless of station of origin or destination. This was initially 4d for a Second Class standing place, or 6d for a First Class seat. The LBR was locally dubbed 'The Fourpenny Rope', and soon become the subject of a music hall song.

To reduce rope twisting, the LBR built chambers beneath the tracks, close to the winding engines, where men, known as 'Clippers', would guide the ropes with large wooden shears. (The Pictorial Times)

Unfortunately, the terminus at Minories was too early to have been photographed when still in use, but this line engraving gives a good impression of its appearance, with low-height 'platforms', and winding drums between the running rails. (The Penny Paper)

On 2nd August 1841, the short extension into Fenchurch Street was opened to the public. It was the first station to be built within the City of London, and the Authorising Act stipulated that it was not to be used on Sundays or certain religious holidays. To appease the Corporation, the Company agreed to clad the Minories bridge with wooden sides and slate roof. Therefore, when it was reported to Parliament that the trains were not visible from below, the Act was repealed, and services had unrestricted use of Fenchurch Street.

The LBR began to experiment with a small amount of goods traffic in 1842, and constructed some temporary depots, including one at Crutched Friars, but the scheme was not destined for success, and after a short time was abandoned.

In 1845, the Company announced its intention of constructing an extension from Stepney to Epping. This would have entailed a junction with the Eastern Counties Railway near Bow, and the use of ECR tracks as far as Stratford. The Eastern Counties objected to this however, and despite an offer from the LBR that some of their trains could use Fenchurch Street as a return gesture, they refused to allow running rights into Stratford. Eventually, a tenuous agreement was reached between the two companies, which allowed the LBR to construct the

section between Stepney and Bow, on the condition that the Eastern Counties had sole rights to the Epping scheme.

Like the Blackwall system, the ECR had been built to a gauge of 5ft, but this was altered to standard in 1844. Therefore, before the connection could be made, the LBR metals had to be re-laid, and authorisation to do so was duly provided by Acts of 1845 and 1846.

The Company then went ahead with the job of conversion, and constructing the new line towards Bow. In the meantime, the LBR opened negotiations with the recently formed East & West India Docks & Birmingham Junction Railway, regarding the possibility of these newcomers using Fenchurch Street as their City terminus. This new line had been promoted to provide the London & North Western Railway with a direct route from the West Midlands to the India group of docks, and although primarily intended for freight traffic, its promoters were beginning to think about introducing a local passenger service as well. Naturally the Blackwall Directors were enthusiastic about this proposal, but in their haste to reach an agreement, they managed to upset the Eastern Counties, and any thoughts of Blackwall trains being allowed to run into Stratford had to be shelved.

The era of non-standard gauge, and cable haulage on the London & Blackwall came to an end on 14th February 1849, when locomotives began to operate the line on the north side of the formation. Work on reducing the width of the 'south line' started immediately, and was completed by the beginning of April. The LBR, for nine years a somewhat enigmatic curiosity, now became an integrated part of the growing London railway network, although for many years the viaduct alongside Regent's Canal Dock had to covered with a light iron roof to protect ships from locomotive sparks.

The new line from Stepney to Bow was known as the Blackwall Extension Railway, but although a useful link, its early fortunes were marred by the bad relationship which existed between the LBR and the ECR. An interchange station was erected near Fairfield Road, and named Victoria Park & Bow, but this was doomed by company politics, and ceased to be used by LBR trains once the East & West India Docks & Birmingham Junction passenger service started in September 1850.

A further use for the new line manifested itself when the London Tilbury & Southend Extension Railway was mooted in 1851. Presumably the relationship between the LBR and the ECR must have defrosted somewhat, as the venture was to be constructed by both companies as a joint project. It was authorised by an Act of Parliament dated 17th June 1852, and stretched from a junction east of Forest Gate, on the Eastern Counties line, through Barking to Tilbury and Southend.

It was proposed to run the new service with trains from Fenchurch Street (LBR) and Shoreditch (ECR), and couple both together when they met at Stratford. This would mean an extra strain on the already busy tracks between Stepney and the City, so a complete rebuilding of Fenchurch Street was undertaken, together with an extra line to the north of the existing formation. On 1st January 1853, whilst the work of widening the viaduct was taking place, the East & West India Docks & Birmingham Junction Railway changed its name to the much less cumbersome, and more appropriate 'North London Railway'. Shortly afterwards, the LNWR began to use this line to bring freight into the City, and constructed a new goods depot

at Haydon Square, near the Minories. The Royal Assent had been given for this on 5th June 1851, and the premises were brought into use on 12th March 1853.

The London, Tilbury & Southend Railway, now short of the 'Extension' part of its title, was opened from Forest Gate Junction to Tilbury on 13th April 1854. The trains were worked as originally proposed, with the down Fenchurch Street and Shoreditch portions combining at Stratford, and the corresponding up services dividing at the same place. From 3rd July 1854, the joint Board of Directors leased the line to its builders, Peto, Brassey & Betts.

Because of the hefty job of viaduct widening, the new track west of Stepney, which was to be used as an additional up line took a long time to complete, but was finally ready for use in 1856.

Once the LTSR was fully operational, it became apparent that the route via Forest Gate was less than ideal. Therefore it decided to build a new line between Barking and Bow to give their trains a more direct route into Fenchurch Street. This was authorised by an Act of 7th July 1856, and joined the Blackwall Extension Railway slightly north-east of the connection already used by NLR services at Bow Common.

Traffic over the route continued to increase, with new spurs providing links with other railways at Abbey Mills and Bow. These were served by both passenger and freight trains, and eventually the approaches to Fenchurch Street hosted no less than six goods depots..

In 1862, the ECR joined forces with various other companies to form the Great Eastern Railway, and three years later, the management agreed to lease their line to the GER for a period of 999 years.

The GER explored the possibility of diverting more of their suburban traffic over the line, but decided against it as they felt that the facilities were already over-stretched. From 1st January 1869, NLR trains ceased to operate into Fenchurch Street, but a shuttle to and from Bow (NLR) was retained as the service was handed over to the Great Eastern.

The 1880s saw further growth for the LTSR, with new lines being constructed at the Essex end of its system.

It had long been a cause of concern to the LTSR that they had to rely on another company's City terminus for the success of their operations, and as their passenger traffic continued to increase, it was clear that the facilities at Fenchurch Street were becoming inadequate. They therefore began to look around to see if it would be possible to divert some of their services elsewhere, and in August 1890 received an Act to construct a new line linking East Ham and Barking with South Tottenham. This was undertaken as a joint venture with the Midland Railway, and allowed LTSR trains access to St. Pancras. The route was known as the Tottenham & Forest Gate Railway, and it opened in 1894..

Despite this, the majority of LTS services continued to work into Fenchurch Street, and overcrowding of the approach tracks again became acute. Therefore, a further widening of the viaduct was carried out, and an additional down line provided in 1896.

Another intended cure for the hold-ups was the Whitechapel & Bow line, which was jointly promoted by the LTS and Metropolitan District Railways. This was authorised in 1897. It commenced at Campbell Road Junction, west of Bromley station, then descended at a ruling gradient of 1 in 40 into a cut and cover tunnel, which continued to an end-on connection with the MDR at Whitechapel. It was formally opened on Saturday 31st May 1902. It was originally steam worked, but this was only intended to be temporary, as an Act authorising electrification was passed on 31st July, just two month after opening.

To cope with the extra traffic, the LTSR decided to quadruple their line between Campbell Road Junction and the sidings at Little Ilford, near East Ham. They received authorisation for the section from Plaistow to East Ham in 1898 prior to the opening of the W&B, but took no further action until 1902, when Powers were granted for the remaining stretch. Work commenced on widening the formation, and rebuilding the stations, and by August 1905, all had been completed. This was only an interim measure however, as a scheme to extend both quadrupling and electrification to Barking had already been sanctioned.

Despite its continuing success, it perhaps seemed likely that one day the LTSR would be absorbed by the Great Eastern. However, this was not to be, as on 7th August 1912 an Act was passed which allowed it to be acquired by the Midland Railway.

After World War I, many of the country's railways were in a run-down condition, both physically and financially, and the most logical remedy was to reduce the number of companies, by grouping them together. This took affect from 1st January 1923, with the GER becoming part of the London & North Eastern Railway, whilst the MR was absorbed into the London Midland & Scottish Railway.

Services were little altered at first, but three years later, the ailing Blackwall line was earmarked for closure. A withdrawal date was set for 30th June 1926, but because of the General Strike, trains ceased to run after 3rd May.

Fenchurch Street now had less services to accommodate, but it was still prone to overcrowding. Therefore a major rebuilding scheme was announced, whereby the existing platforms would be replaced by a pair of new islands, and colour-light signalling installed. The work started in 1932, and by April 1935, the various station alterations had been completed.

In 1936, the LNER announced its intentions to electrify the line between Liverpool Street and Shenfield, and also include the section from Fenchurch Street to Bow Junction. Work on this scheme was started, but was then delayed by the onset of World War II. When it recommenced, much of east London was left in ruins following bombing.

Following nationalisation in 1948, and the formation of British Railways, the work continued, but the section from Stratford into Fenchurch Street was dropped from the electrification scheme, and closed instead. This meant that the only regular passenger trains now using the ex-LBR City terminus, were those off the former LTSR, which like a cuckoo in the nest had finally inherited the entire station.

Under nationalisation, the section between Fenchurch Street and Gas Factory Junction became part of the Eastern Region, whilst the LTS line proper was taken by the London

Midland. This was to change soon afterwards however, as from 20th February 1949, the whole route was handed over to the Eastern.

Despite being closed to regular traffic, the line to Stratford was eventually electrified, so that it could be used as an emergency route, but LTS line passenger remained steam worked for over a decade more. In the late 1950s, work began on the installation of 25kV overhead wiring, and at the same time, the old LNER system of 1500vDC from Stratford was altered accordingly. The first Southend line electric made its debut at Fenchurch Street on 6th November 1961, and steam finally bowed out after June the following year.

In 1981, the Government announced a scheme to redevelop around eight square miles of the East End, and set up the London Docklands Development Corporation. This was to breathe new life into an area which had been largely empty since the demise of the docks in the previous decade. To ensure the venture was a success, it was decided to build the Docklands Light Railway, which would link the City with the Isle of Dogs and either Mile End or Stratford. In the end, it was Stratford which was chosen as the north-eastern terminus, and the whole system opened to the public on 31st August 1987. The DLR terminus at Tower Gateway stands to the south of the main line, just outside Fenchurch Street, and its tracks parallel the present LTS route to what is now Limehouse station, having taken over part of the existing viaduct. Beyond Limehouse, it diverges onto the old Blackwall formation, and continues towards Westferry, alongside the Regents Canal Dock.

With the dissolution of the nationalised network in the mid-1990s, it was intended that the LTS line should be sold to a management buy-out consortium known as Enterprise Rail. The franchise was duly awarded to this group on 19th December 1995, with the takeover planned for 4th February the following year. However, just hours before this came about, the procedure was stopped due to alleged ticketing irregularities. The franchise then passed to a different group, Prism Rail, who took over operations on 26th May 1996. New rolling stock was ordered, and in December 1997, Railtrack announced that they would be investing £75million on infrastructure improvements.

Therefore with both the LTS and DLR very much part of today's railway network, it seems that a line which started life as an engineering curiosity back in 1840 will continue to play a useful role in the London of tomorrow.

PASSENGER SERVICES

To catalogue the development of these in detail would require an entire volume of tables and statistics, so only a basic outline is given here.

In 1842 the cable-hauled service operated every fifteen minutes from 8.30am until 9.45pm. The journey time by through carriage from end to end was officially thirteen minutes, but it seems that delays due to rope problems were not uncommon.

By 1850, Blackwall trains ran every fifteen minutes from 8.30am until 8pm, and then every half hour until 10pm. From Blackwall, there was a regular service of steamboats to Woolwich and Gravesend, and through bookings were available. Trains for Bow ran at thirty minute intervals, and left Fenchurch Street on the hour, and half-past. All services over the LBR ceased on Sundays between 11am and 1pm in accordance with the accepted hours of worship.

Four years later, with Fenchurch Street becoming ever busier, the Blackwall services continued to run every fifteen minutes, but now had to fit in with ECR, LTSR and NLR trains. The June 1854 Bradshaw showed LTSR departures at seven, twenty-two, and thirty-seven minutes past the hour, which in each case was just two minutes behind an NLR train. At first, LTS services had both Fenchurch Street and Shoreditch portions, which either joined or split at Stratford depending on direction of travel. The ECR terminus at Shoreditch however was inconveniently placed for central London, so most passengers preferred to use Fenchurch Street. The practice of combining and detaching at Stratford ceased in 1856, when the Shoreditch portions were withdrawn.

From March 1858 all LTSR trains from Fenchurch Street were diverted over the new line from Bow Common Junction. A fast journey between Stepney and Barking took seven minutes less than services via Forest Gate Junction, but the saving was somewhat less with stopping trains.

As Fenchurch Street was suffering from congestion, the NLR opened its own terminus at Broad Street in 1865, but it continued to operate a shuttle over the earlier route from Bow for another four years.

The North London also worked services onto the LTSR by way of the Bow - Bromley curve. These started in May 1869, and operated locally between Chalk Farm and Plaistow. There were eight of these trains each day, and most of them connected with existing LTSR services at Plaistow. From 1st October 1871, they ceased to work into Chalk Farm, but turned back at Bow instead. However, following discussions between the two companies, they reverted to Chalk Farm in June 1877, only to be cut back permanently to Bow the following February.

Apart from these local services however, the Bow - Bromley Curve also hosted various through trains which worked to destinations such as Tilbury and Thames Haven. These ran at various times from 1869 onwards, but were withdrawn from the timetable in 1914. In later years, excursions worked over the route, whilst between 1923 and 1935 the curve was used by certain LTS line services which ran into Broad Street, due to overcrowding at Fenchurch Street. The shuttle service between Bow and Plaistow was a casualty of World War I however, and ceased to operate from 1st January 1916.

Throughout the years various Eastern Counties and Great Eastern Railway services worked to and from Fenchurch Street, with those off the North Woolwich and Loughton branches being the earliest. Until 1858, all Woolwich trains ran via Stratford, but afterwards the route through Abbey Mills Junction was preferred. Other destinations reached by GER Fenchurch Street trains included Ilford, Lower Edmonton and the dockside terminus at Gallions.

The first train over the Whitechapel & Bow line operated on 31st May 1902. Electric working east of Whitechapel was brought in on 20th August 1905, and in October the same year, District steam locomotives made their last appearance on the route when the MDR service to Upminster was withdrawn. The District electrification was extended to Barking from 1st April 1908, and continued into Upminster in 1932.

In June 1910, a through service over the W&B line was inaugurated between Ealing Broadway and Southend. The service was withdrawn as a World War II economy measure, and never reinstated.

The first half of the twentieth century saw the demise of GE line services into Fenchurch Street, starting with the trains to and from Blackwall. This line lost its Sunday workings from 4th October 1908, and closed to passenger traffic in May 1926. What remained was either killed off by the Second World War, or else simply phased out. In the latter category comes the Loughton branch, where steam hauled trains were replaced by tube stock, when the route was transferred to the London Transport Central Line in the late 1940s. The final Fenchurch Street service inherited from the Great Eastern was that to Ilford and Gidea Park, which survived the war, but was withdrawn in November 1949.

LTS trains continued through the 1950s much as before, with some calling at various intermediate stations between Stepney East and Barking. This practice stopped following electrification however, when the main line platforms at Bromley, Plaistow, Upton Park and East Ham all fell into disuse.

FENCHURCH STREET

1. We start our journey at Fenchurch Street and see the station frontage as it appeared on 8th July 1950. Despite the passage of two years since nationalisation, the lettering above the windows still proclaimed LNER ownership. The building dates from 1853-4, and was designed by the civil engineer, George Berkeley, in collaboration with architect, William Tite. Its pediment was curved, so that it followed the shape of the single-arch, crescent-truss overall roof, which had a span of 101ft, and length of 300ft. The original awning above the entrance doors was very plain and utilitarian in appearance, but this later collapsed and was replaced by one of standard Great Eastern design as seen here. (H.C. Casserley)

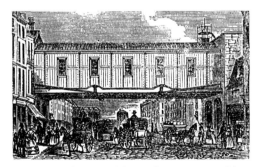

So that trains could not be seen working into the City of London, the authorities insisted that the bridge over Minories had to be completely enclosed. This is how it appeared around 1851. (Illustrated London News)

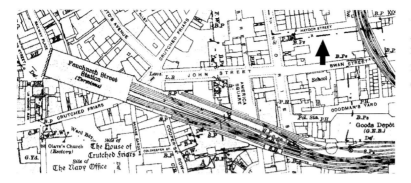

A map of 1913. The goods depot indicated near the bottom right, is Goodmans Yard. *(See pictures 23-25).*

2. Having passed through the entrance doors, we see the booking hall as it appeared in the early 1980s. When rebuilt in 1853, the station was provided with two ticket offices, of which one dealt with London & Blackwall traffic, and the other served the LTSR. There were stairways at either end, and these led up to a small circulating area at the head of the platforms. The separate offices were combined into one in 1932, but no further major alterations were made until a comprehensive rebuilding scheme was implemented soon after this photograph was taken. (J.E. Connor)

4. Moving on from the concourse, we stand on the island platform, numbered 2 and 3, and look back towards the buffer stops. On the left we see a train from Blackwall, which has arrived at No.1, whilst on the engine road to our right stands a locomotive, bearing an Ongar destination board. Next to this is LTSR 4-4-2T No. 57 *Crouch Hill*, which has been relieved of the stock it brought into Platform 4, and will subsequently work a service to Southend. Platform 4 had a length of 765ft, and was used exclusively by LTSR trains. (British Railways)

3.   Having climbed the stairs from the booking hall, we arrive at the concourse, and stand opposite the entrance to platforms 2 and 3 in the early years of the twentieth century. When built in 1841, two platforms were deemed sufficient, but during the rebuilding of 1853, the number was increased to four, and by the time this photograph was taken, a fifth had been added. To the right, alongside the bookstall, we see Platform 1, which had a length of 380ft, and accommodated the Blackwall services. Numbers 2 and 3 referred to a 555ft island, which was used by GER suburban trains, linking the City with destinations such as North Woolwich, Ilford and Loughton. (Lens of Sutton)

5. Having walked to the far end of platforms 2 an 3, we see a Great Eastern train from Ilford arriving, hauled by S44 class 0-4-4T No. 1100, whilst in the middle road stands LTSR 4-4-2T No. 27 *Whitechapel*. Platform 4, seen to the left, became an island at its eastern end, with its other face serving a 470ft bay which was designated No.5. Behind this, in the distance, stands the huge warehouse of Goodmans Yard depot. (Real Photographs)

6. Still at the station's east end, we see LTSR 4-4-2T No. 38 *Westcliff* standing in the middle road, with a GER locomotive behind. The large building seen to the right accommodated both LBR and LTSR offices, and dated from 1881. This was equipped with its own booking office in John Street, which was linked to platforms 4 and 5 by means of direct stairs. The delightfully local names carried by these engines were removed after the LTSR was taken over by the Midland Railway in 1912. (LCGB Ken Nunn Collection)

7. Platform 4, being the longest, provided an ideal vantage point for viewing train movements around the station. In this photograph, which was taken on 22nd August 1926, we see a class F4 2-4-2T No.7106 simmering to the left, and *Tilbury Tank* No. 2116 waiting in the middle road. This engine started life as LTSR No.7 *Barking*, and remained in service until September 1935. (H.C. Casserley)

LONDON and BLACKWALL.—Great Eastern.

LONDON, TILBURY, and SOUTHEND. [Eng. & Gen. Man., A. L. Stride.

August 1881

Since the 1850s, Fenchurch Street had suffered from overcrowding, and despite various alterations and improvements made over the years, its restricted facilities continued to cause problems. As traffic continued to grow, the only platform long enough to accommodate LTS line trains was No.4, and this seriously hampered the station's usefulness. Therefore a £250,000 scheme to modernise the premises was announced in 1932, and work set about its rebuilding. The old platforms were removed, and replaced by a pair of new islands. That which comprised faces 1 and 2 had a length of 550ft, whilst 3 and 4 measured 750ft. Here we see diagrams of the station, as it was before modernising *(above)*, and as it appeared afterwards *(below)*. The work was completed in April 1935. (Railway Magazine)

8. This is the signal box which was gantried over the up slow line, opposite the end of platforms 4 and 5. It had a Saxby & Farmer frame, and at the time of its demise was equipped with 115 working levers. It was closed on 14th April 1935, and replaced by a new 140-lever box, when colour light signalling was introduced. (British Rail)

9. At the time of rebuilding, passenger access to the platforms was also improved by the enlargement of the concourse. This was achieved by the demolition of various buildings, such as the old telegraph office which we saw in photograph 3. At the same time new barrier gates were installed, together with clocks which indicated departure times. This arrangement proved more satisfactory, and survived until the major rebuilding scheme of the 1980s. Here we see the concourse as it appeared in the 1960s. (Stations UK)

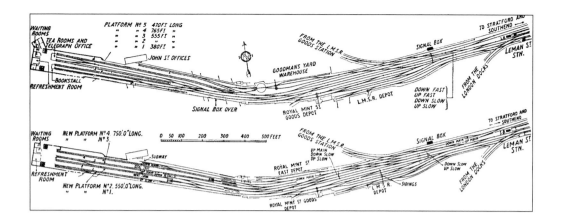

London Tilbury and Southend Railway.

Fenchurch Street
TO
Dagenham Dock

10. The rebuilding also resulted in the demolition of the tea rooms which once backed onto platforms 3 and 4. These were replaced by a swish new waiting room and cafeteria which was built very much in the art-deco style of its period. This stood on the north side of the concourse, and is seen here in the early 1980s, shortly before it was removed. The current buffet is located on the opposite side of the station. (J.E. Connor)

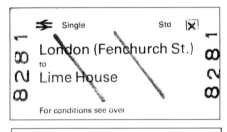

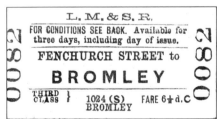

LONDON TO SOUTHEND-ON-SEA AND SHOEBURYNESS.

1	London (St. Pancras)............dep.																					
2	Kentish Town .... "																					
3	Fenchurch Street............dep.	4 25	5 0		5 37				6 45	6 55	7 30		8 4		8 12	9 8	9 12	9 41		
4	Stepney East		5 6		5 43					7 1	7 36		8 11		8 18	9 14		9 47		
5	Burdett Road																			
6	Bromley				5 48			6 55								9 25				
7	Plaistow		5 15		5 54			7 1		7 44		8 20		8 27		9 30	9 56		
8	Upton Park				5 58			7 5		7 48		8 24		8 31		9 34	10 0		
9	East Ham		5 20		6 3			7 9	7 14	7 52		8 28		8 35	9 25	9 39	10 4		
10	Barking	4 40	5 27	5 32	6 12			7 1	7 14	7 21	7 58		8 34		8 41	9 32	9 47	10 9		
11	Becontree												8 40				9 53			
12	Dagenham		5 36										8 45				9 58			
13	Hornchurch		5 42										8 51				10 4			
14	Upminster		5 48			7 1	7 8					8 29	8 57				10 11			
15	East Horndon		5 56				7 16						9 5				10 19			
16	Laindon	5 8	6 6				7 25						9 15				10 29			
17	Dagenham Dock.....................			5 38	6 19			7 8	7 21	7 28	8 5				8 48	9 39		10 16		
18	Rainham				6 24			7 13	7 26	7 33	8 10				8 53	9 44		10 21		
19	Purfleet Rifle Range Halt.....................														8 59	9 50		10 27		
20	Purfleet				6 32				7 33	7 40	8 17				9 4	9 53		10 30		
21	Grays				6 42	7 19		7 28	7 42	7 49	8 26	8 47			9 14	10 2		10 39		
22	Tilbury Town (for Tilbury Docks) ...				6 50	7 24		7 33	7 48	7 55	8 32	8 52			9 20	10 8		10 45		
23	Tilbury (Riverside)..................arr.				6 53	7 27		7 36	7 51	7 58	8 35	8 55			9 23	10 11		10 48		
24	Gravesend (Town Pier)............arr.				7 5	7 39		7 46	8 3	8 10	8 50	9 7			9 40	10 24		11 0		
25	Do. do. ....dep.				6 40			7 44								10 4				
26	Tilbury (Riverside)..................dep.				6 57			7 56								10 16				
27	Low Street				7 3			8 2								10 24				
28	East Tilbury Halt				7 6			8 5								10 28				
29	Stanford-le-Hope.....................				7 14			8 12								10 32				
30	Pitsea (for Vange)............dep.	5 18	6 14		7 24		7 34		8 23				9 23			10 44	10 37			
31	Benfleet (for Canvey Island)	5 25	6 21		7 31		7 41		8 30				9 30			10 51	10 44			
32	Leigh-on-Sea	5 36	6 28		7 38		7 48		8 37				9 37			10 58	10 51			
33	Chalkwell	5 41	6 33		7 43		7 53		8 41				9 42			11 3	10 56			
34	Westcliff-on-Sea	5 49	6 37		7 47		7 57		8 45				9 46			11 7	11 0			
35	Southend-on-Sea.....................	5 53	6 44		7 54		8 2		8 50				9 52			11 13	11 5			
36	Southend East	6 1	6 52		8 1		8 8						9 58			11 20	11 11			
37	Thorpe Bay	6 5	6 56		8 5		8 12		8 58				10 2			11 24	11 15			
38	Shoeburyness ....arr.	6 11	7 0		8 9		8 16		9 2				10 6			11 28	11 19			

		SO		SO	SX	SO			SX	SX	SO	SX	SX	SO	SX		SX	¶ SX	SX	SX
1	London (St. Pancras)............dep.																				
2	Kentish Town .... "																				
3	Fenchurch Street............dep.	2 12		2 32	3 8	3 8	3 25	3 45	4 7		4 15	4 26	4 26			4 45	5 4	5 8	5 15	
4	Stepney East	2 18		2 38	3 14	3 14	3 31		4 13		4 21	4 32	4 32			4 51		5 14	5 21	
5	Burdett Road																			
6	Bromley			2 47			3 39													
7	Plaistow																			
8	Upton Park			2 52	3 24		3 44													
9	East Ham			2 58	3 30	3 26	3 50	4 1	4 26	4 30	4 33	4 45	4 45			5 3		5 25	5 34	
10	Barking	2 30																		
11	Becontree																			
12	Dagenham																			
13	Hornchurch																			
14	Upminster	2 45	2 57	3 13	3 45	3 41		4 16	4 14	4 44		4 58	4 59	5 5	5 5	6 5	18	5 34	5 49	
15	East Horndon			3 21	3 53					4 52		5 7	5 12			5 33				
16	Laindon	3 0		3 31	4 3	3 56		4 31	4 58	5 2		5 17	5 21			5 33			6 4	
17	Dagenham Dock.....................						3 57				4 40							5 31		
18	Rainham						4 2				4 45							5 36		
19	Purfleet Rifle Range Halt.....................						4 8				4 51									
20	Purfleet						4 11				4 54							5 43		
21	Grays			3 14			4 20				5 3					5 24		5 52		
22	Tilbury Town (for Tilbury Docks)...			3 19			4 26				5 9					5 29		5 57		
23	Tilbury (Riverside)..................arr.			3 22			4 29				5 12					5 32		6 0		
24	Gravesend (Town Pier)............arr.			3 39			4 41				5 25					5 50		6 12		
25	Do. do. ....dep.						4 20				4 53							5 45		
26	Tilbury (Riverside)..................dep.						4 33				5 16							6 3		
27	Low Street						4 39				5 22									
28	East Tilbury Halt						4 42				5 25							6 11		
29	Stanford-le-Hope.....................						4 49				5 33							6 18		
30	Pitsea (for Vange) ....dep.	3 9		3 39	4 11	4 5	4 59	4 40	5 6	5 9	5 47		5 26	5 28		5 41		6 27	6 13	
31	Benfleet (for Canvey Island).....................	3 16		3 46	4 18	4 12	5 6	4 47	5 13		5 54	5 20	5 33			5 48			6 20	
32	Leigh-on-Sea	3 23		3 53	4 25	4 19	5 13	4 54	5 20		6 1	5 27	5 40			5 55	6 6		6 27	
33	Chalkwell	3 28		3 58	4 30	4 24	5 18	4 59	5 25		6 6	5 32	5 45			6 0	6 11		6 32	
34	Westcliff-on-Sea.....................	3 32		4 2	4 34	4 28	5 22	5 3	5 29		6 10	5 36	5 49			6 4	6 15		6 36	
35	Southend-on-Sea.....................	3 37		4 7	4 39	4 33	5 27	5 8	5 34		6 15	5 41	5 54			6 9	6 20		6 41	
36	Southend East	3 42		4 13	4 45	4 39	5 32	5 14	5 39			5 47	6 0			6 14	6 26		6 47	
37	Thorpe Bay	3 46		4 17	4 49	4 43	5 36	5 18	5 43			5 51	6 4			6 18	6 30		6 51	
38	Shoeburyness ....arr.	3 50		4 21	4 53	4 47	5 40	5 22	5 47			5 55	6 8			6 22	6 34		6 55	

SO—Saturdays only.   SX—Saturdays excepted.

¶—Conveys First and Third Class passengers.

Extracts from morning and afternoon timetables for October 1942.

11.   The original Shenfield electrification scheme included the section of line between Bow Junction and Fenchurch Street. This was abandoned before completion however, but later wired so that it could be used in emergencies. Here we look towards the buffer stops on 16th May 1959, and see the overhead 1500vDC wires above the tracks serving platforms 1 and 2. (F. Church)

12.   We now stand beneath the arched overall roof, and see trains on platforms 1 and 4, with their locomotives resting at the buffer stops. The engine to the left is one of William Stanier's 3-cylinder 4MT class 2-6-4Ts, which were introduced in 1934 specifically for the LTS line. (Stations UK)

13. Still looking towards the buffer stops, we have a good view of the canopies which were erected during the 1935 rebuilding. A bunker-first BR Standard 2-6-4T awaits departure with her train from platform 2, whilst Stanier 3-cylinder class 4MT 2-6-4T No. 42506 stands at platform 3. Although the 1500vDC overhead wires were never used by scheduled passenger services, empty electric units often ran at off-peak times to keep them clean. (F. Church)

14. From a vantage point just east of the platforms we see BR Standard class 4MT No.80103 departing with the 1.25pm to Shoeburyness on 22nd August 1960. This loco was the first of her class to be scrapped, being withdrawn in 1962. (F. Church)

CHEAP DAY RETURN TICKETS

ANY DAY   ANY TRAIN

FROM

FENCHURCH STREET

TO	RETURN FARES		TO	RETURN FARES	
	First class	Third class		First class	Third class
	s. d.	s. d.		s. d.	s. d.
Benfleet	9 0	6 0	Southend-on-Sea ... (Central)	9 5	6 3
Chalkwell	9 0	6 0	Southend-on-Sea ... (East)	9 9	6 6
Leigh-on-Sea	9 0	6 0	Thorpe Bay ...	10 2	6 9
Shoeburyness... ...	10 6	7 0	Westcliff-on-Sea ...	9 5	6 3

CHEAP DAY RETURN TICKETS

ANY DAY

TO

FENCHURCH STREET

AVAILABILITY
OUTWARD

MONDAYS TO FRIDAYS—BY ANY TRAIN AT OR AFTER 9.0 a.m.
SATURDAYS AND SUNDAYS—BY ANY TRAIN

RETURN

BY ANY TRAIN ON DAY OF ISSUE

FROM	RETURN FARES		FROM	RETURN FARES	
	First class	Third class		First class	Third class
	s. d.	s. d.		s. d.	s. d.
Benfleet	9 0	6 0	Southend-on-Sea ... (Central)	9 5	6 3
Chalkwell	9 0	6 0	Southend-on-Sea ... (East)	9 9	6 6
Leigh-on-Sea	9 0	6 0	Thorpe Bay ...	10 2	6 9
Pitsea	9 0	6 0	Westcliff-on-Sea ...	9 5	6 3
Shoeburyness ...	10 6	7 0			

Passengers may alight at a station short of destination in either direction upon surrender of the ticket, and commence the return journey from an intermediate station.

CONDITIONS OF ISSUE

These tickets are issued subject to the British Transport Commission's published Regulations and Conditions applicable to British Railways exhibited at their stations or obtainable free of charge at station booking offices.

LUGGAGE ALLOWANCES are as set out in these general notices.

Children under three years of age, free; three years and under fourteen half-fares.

September 1955

15. The old London Tilbury & Southend Railway had a liking for decorating locomotives for special occasions, and to a certain extent this tradition carried on into BR days. Here, highly polished Standard class 4MT 2-6-4T No. 80135 is seen departing from platform 4 with a P&O Shareholders' train to Tilbury. (British Rail)

16. Looking east from the station on 15th September 1958, we witness classmate No. 80133 running light towards platform 2 in readiness to haul a train out bunker-first. The 1935 signal box can just be seen above the tracks in the middle distance. (F. Church)

17.   Although ex-Great Eastern locomotives ceased to run into Fenchurch Street on a regular basis in 1949, they still made the odd appearance on special trains until the end of steam. Here we record class N7/4 0-6-2T No. 69614 awaiting departure with the Railway Correspondence & Travel Society Hertfordshire Railtour on 27th April 1958. This locomotive was employed as West Side station pilot at Liverpool Street from 1956 until her withdrawal in 1960, and was always kept in immaculate condition. (D. Lawrence)

18. The empty electric trains which operated into Fenchurch Street to keep the wires clean appear to have been seldom photographed, but here we see two units, headed by No. 058 passing Standard class 4MT 2-6-4T No.80104, as they set out on their return run to Ilford depot. (British Rail)

19. Electric services made their debut on the LTS line proper on 6th November 1961. Here we witness the first up train passing beneath the 1935 signal box as it approaches Fenchurch Street. This box remained in use until 22nd July 1994, when it was rendered redundant by a new signalling centre at Upminster. The building to the extreme right, partially hidden by coaching stock, is the former Midland Railway hydraulic accumulator tower, which was once part of the old City Goods Station. (British Rail)

20. The 6.10pm to Southend departs from Fenchurch Street behind Stanier 3-cylinder class 4MT 2-6-4T No.42501 on Friday 15th June 1962. This was the last peak-hour steam working on the LTS via Upminster, and the locomotive was specially provided with a traditional destination board, which had not been in common use for a number of years. The full electric service started three days later, and the line's steam locomotives were either withdrawn or transferred elsewhere. (British Rail)

21. Steam may have disappeared in 1962, but Fenchurch Street station remained largely in its 1935 condition for around two decades longer. Here we stand on platform 3, and look towards the buffer stops sometime in the 1960s, with the new electric units very much in evidence. The canopies and George Berkeley's historic overall roof disappeared in the 1980s, when an office development was constructed above the platforms. (Stations UK)

22. The Docklands Light Railway terminus at Tower Gateway adjoins the south side of the former Blackwall viaduct. In this 1994 view we can see two DLR trains awaiting departure, with the platform ends of Fenchurch Street curving off to our right. (J.E. Connor)

CHEAP DAY RETURN TICKETS
ANY DAY   ANY TRAIN
TO
BENFLEET   LEIGH-ON-SEA
CHALKWELL WESTCLIFF-ON-SEA
SOUTHEND-ON-SEA
THORPE BAY   SHOEBURYNESS

RETURN FARES—THIRD CLASS

FROM	To Benfleet	To Leigh-on-Sea	To Chalkwell	To Westcliff-on-Sea / Southend-on-Sea (Central)	To Southend-on-Sea (East)	To Thorpe Bay	To Shoeburyness
	s. d.	s. d.	s. d.	s. d.	s. d.	s. d.	s. d.
*Barking	—	5 6	5 6	5 9	6 0	6 3	6 6
Becontree	—	5 6	5 6	5 9	6 0	6 3	6 6
Black Horse Road	6 0	6 0	6 0	6 3	6 6	6 9	7 0
Bromley	6 0	6 0	6 0	6 3	6 6	6 9	7 0
Crouch Hill	6 6	6 6	6 6	6 9	7 0	7 3	7 6
Dagenham East	—	—	5 6	5 9	6 0	6 3	6 6
Dagenham Heathway	—	5 6	5 6	5 9	6 0	6 3	6 6
East Ham	5 6	5 9	5 9	6 0	6 3	6 6	6 9
Elm Park	—	5 0	5 0	5 0	6 0	6 3	6 6
Harringay Park	6 3	6 3	6 3	6 6	6 9	7 0	7 3
Kentish Town	6 9	6 9	6 9	7 0	7 3	7 6	7 9
Leyton Midland Road	5 9	5 9	5 9	6 0	6 3	6 6	6 9
Leytonstone High Road	5 9	5 9	5 9	6 0	6 3	6 6	6 9
Plaistow	5 9	5 9	5 9	6 0	6 3	6 6	6 9
St. Pancras	6 9	6 9	6 9	7 0	7 3	7 6	7 9
South Tottenham	6 0	6 0	6 0	6 3	6 6	6 9	7 0
*Stepney (East)	6 0	6 0	6 0	6 3	6 6	6 9	7 0
Upney	—	5 6	5 6	5 9	6 0	6 3	6 6
Upper Holloway	6 6	6 6	6 6	6 9	7 0	7 3	7 6
Upton Park	5 6	5 9	5 9	6 0	6 3	6 6	6 9
Walthamstow	6 0	6 0	6 0	6 3	6 6	6 9	7 0
Wanstead Park	5 9	5 9	5 9	6 0	6 3	6 6	6 9
West Ham (Manor Road)	5 9	5 9	5 9	6 0	6 3	6 6	6 9
Woodgrange Park	5 9	5 9	5 9	6 0	6 3	6 6	6 9

* First class tickets will also be issued at approximately 50 per cent. over the third class fares where First Class accommodation is available.

Passengers may alight at a station short of destination in either direction upon surrender of the ticket, and commence the return journey from an intermediate station.

CONDITIONS OF ISSUE

These tickets are issued subject to the British Transport Commission's published Regulations and Conditions applicable to British Railways exibited at their stations or obtainable free of charge at station booking offices.

LUGGAGE ALLOWANCES are as set out in these general notices.

Children under three years of age, free; three years and under fourteen, half-fares.

September 1955

GOODMANS YARD

24. The depot was constructed to deal with ECR and LTSR traffic, and opened in 1861. In this view, we are looking west, and see the large depot warehouse on the right. The close proximity to Fenchurch Street is emphasised by the fact that the station signal box can be seen near the centre of the photograph, just beyond the two locomotives. The corrugated iron archway leading into the warehouse sheltered the commencement of a siding, which lay at approximately ninety degrees to the running lines, and was reached by way of a wagon turntable. Inside there was a wagon hoist, which allowed trucks to be lowered to street level for loading and unloading. On the opposite side of the line lay the GNR depot at Royal Mint Street, but unfortunately all we can see of this here are some of its sidings. (British Rail)

23. Here we are looking into the depot entrance. Like so much of the East End, it was badly damaged by the Luftwaffe during World War II, although it was not officially closed until April 1951. (British Rail)

25. 4-4-2T No. 18 *Burdett Road* gets into her stride on 12th July 1913, as she passes the huge Goodmans Yard warehouse with a Fenchurch Street to Southend train formed of four-wheeled stock. After the Midland takeover in 1912, locomotives still bearing LTSR livery and names became somewhat of a rarity, as the new owners were eager to repaint them in their own colours. The Roman Catholic Church of the English Martyrs, seen to the right, adjoined the commencement of the short branch to Haydon Square goods depot, which was opened by the London & North Western Railway in 1853. (K. Nunn / LCGB)

ROYAL MINT STREET

26. According to the writer H.L. Hopwood, the building seen here was adapted from the original Minories terminus of the London & Blackwall Railway. However, by the time this photograph was taken, it had become very much part of Royal Mint Street goods depot. This was originally opened as Minories in 1853, but soon had its name changed to Mint Street. It once dealt with ECR and LTSR traffic, but this was transferred to Goodmans Yard in 1861, when Mint Street became leased to the Great Northern Railway. Around 1870, it was received its final name, Royal Mint Street. (H.L. Hopwood / LCGB)

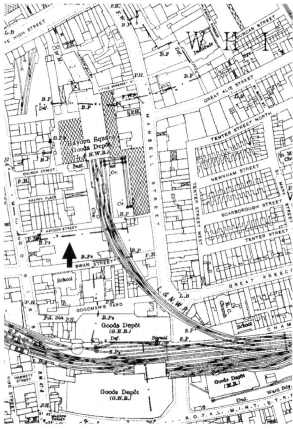

This map shows the goods depots immediately east of Fenchurch Street in 1913. At the bottom left we see Goodmans Yard to the north of the line, with Royal Mint Street opposite. To the right of this lies the Midland Railway City Goods Station, whilst the branch curving northwards is that serving Haydon Square.

CITY GOODS

27. On 29th December 1940, Royal Mint Street depot was badly damaged in an air-raid. Here we see the frontage two months later, after partial demolition had taken place to ensure the structure was safe. The man walking with a determined stride, appears to be heading for the pub next door! The depot officially closed in 1951. (British Rail)

28. Adjoining Royal Mint Street depot was the Midland Railway City Goods Station. This opened in 1862, and closed in 1949. It was later largely demolished, but the red-brick hydraulic accumulator tower seen here still survived in 1998 and had become a listed structure. The Docklands Light Railway utilises part of the depot site, as it dives from viaduct into tunnel en-route to its terminus at Bank. (J.E. Connor)

HAYDON SQUARE

29. This is a view of Haydon Square Junction, looking west in 1922. The signal box was equipped with forty-five levers, and took its share of controlling traffic on the approaches to Fenchurch Street, as well as serving the goods depot from which it took its name. The box was abolished in 1935, after being made redundant by the Fenchurch Street resignalling project. Just beyond the signal gantry, we see the Haydon Square branch diverging to the right, whilst the passenger lines continuing directly ahead. Goodmans Yard warehouse is clearly visible in the middle distance, with the sidings of Royal Mint Street opposite. (British Rail)

30. Here we observe an English Electric Type 1 Bo-Bo diesel locomotive awaiting to depart from Haydon Square depot, on its last day. The branch was promoted by the London & North Western Railway, and received the Royal Assent on 5th June 1851. It opened on 12th March 1853, and was the first LNWR goods station to serve the City. Some of its importance was lost in 1868 however, when better sited freight facilities were brought into use at Broad Street. Nevertheless, Haydon Square continued to play a useful role well into the twentieth century, and remained in use until 2nd July 1962. For some years after closure, a white-on-maroon British Railways nameboard survived above an entrance passageway on the south side of Aldgate High Street, adjoining the bus station, but this finally disappeared in the 1970s. The site has now been redeveloped, although a derelict fragment of viaduct on the east side of Mansell Street continues to mark where the branch once commenced. (D. Lawrence)

LEMAN STREET

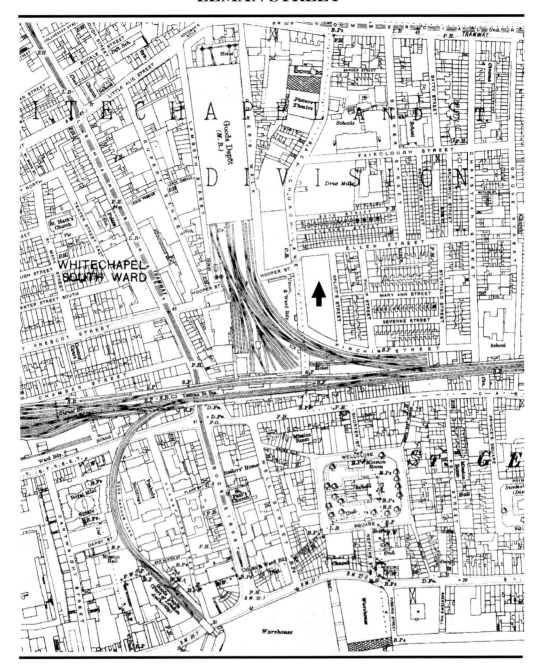

The Ordnance Survey map of 1913 shows the densely built-up area surrounding Leman Street station, and the nearby goods depots. To the north we see the former LTSR establishment at Commercial Road, whilst to the south is East Smithfield. Leman Street station was originally built in 1873, but because clearances were deemed insufficient the Board of Trade refused to sanction its opening. Various alterations therefore had to be made, and it finally opened on 1st June 1877.

31. The Great Eastern E22 0-6-0Ts, or J65s as they later became, were once a common sight on former LBR metals. This is No. 7249 departing from Leman Street with the 12.05pm train from Blackwall on 28th March 1925. The station was provided with two platforms, and these served the slow lines on the south side of the viaduct. (K. Nunn / LCGB)

GREAT EASTERN RAILWAY.
Issued subject to Regulations in the Company's Time Tables.

LEMAN STREET to
Leman St   Leman St
SHADWELL
Shadwell [& St GEORGES EAST] Shadwell
1d   Fare   1d
Third Class

7182   7182

32. Here we can admire No.156 of the same class at the station with the 1.50pm Blackwall - Fenchurch Street on 28th March 1925. The warehouses in the background were still standing in 1998. (K.Nunn / LCGB)

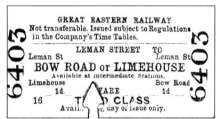

33. The station was reconstructed in connection with the 1895 widening, and provided with a new street level building. Here we are looking from beneath the bridge over Leman Street around 1930, and see the entrance to the left, with Cable Street beyond. Cable Street runs parallel with the line, and derived its name to the form of traction originally employed. The LMSR horse-drawn van adds a nice period touch. (J.E. Connor Collection)

34. In May 1929, an ex-Great Northern Railway N2 0-6-2T was transferred to Stratford for working on the GE Section, and was soon followed by other members of the her class. This is one of them, No. 4723, fitted with a Westinghouse pump, and standing at Leman Street with a Fenchurch Street to Ilford train in the early 1930s. The station was one of a number closed by the GER as a wartime economy from 22nd May 1916, but it reopened three years later. (J.E. Connor Collection)

35. Standing at the west end of the down platform, we see class J65 No.155 with a train from Blackwall in early LNER days. This locomotive, in common with some others in her class, had the front sections of the coupling rods removed, and was therefore running as a 2-4-0T. (Lens of Sutton)

36. Turning in the opposite direction, we see the forty-lever signal box on the right, and the 350yd double-track goods branch to East Smithfield diverging to the left. The box was abolished under the Fenchurch Street resignalling project of 1935, and the station closed six years later. (British Rail)

EAST SMITHFIELD

37. This depot was constructed by the London & Blackwall Railway, and opened on 17th June 1864. The line originally stretched to the north side of Upper East Smithfield, but was extended to the London Docks Wool Warehouse in September of the following year. The facilities here comprised a pair of short sidings, whilst the main buildings were located north of the road. The depot was equipped with a hoist, by which wagons could be lowered from the viaduct to street level for unloading. In 1880 East Smithfield was leased to the London & St. Katherine's Dock Company, who used it for receiving merchandise by road, and forwarding it to the new Royal Albert Dock by rail. Our view is taken from the north end of the depot in

June 1921, and shows a GER 0-6-0T locomotive standing on the bridge over New Martin Street. Behind it we see the upper part of Royal Albert Buildings, a five-storey block of flats erected as a philanthropic venture by Baron Alfred Charles de-Rothschild in 1884. Such developments were intended to rehouse people from the overcrowded East End slums, and a number still survive, although Royal Albert Buildings succumbed to the bulldozer in 1971. East Smithfield depot was extensively rebuilt in 1930, and remained in use until September 1966. It was demolished after closure, and the last surviving section of viaduct near the former junction disappeared with the advent of the Docklands Light Railway. (British Rail)

CHRISTIAN STREET JUNCTION

38. Christian Street Junction was where the LTSR Commercial Road goods branch left the main line and diverged northwards. Here we have a busy scene photographed on 16th May 1959, with an up train hauled by a bunker-first ex-LMS Fairburn 2-6-4T, about to pass BR Standard 2-6-4T No.80077, as diesel-mechanical 0-6-0 No.11503 shunts wagons in the Commercial Road sidings. Between the locomotives we can just see the remains of Leman Street station. This was partially demolished in 1950, although the buildings survived largely intact for a further five years or so. When these were removed, the down platform also disappeared, so only the up side remained.This lingered into the 1980s, and the lower courses of its brickwork could still be seen in 1998 beneath the concrete trackbed of the Docklands Light Railway. (F. Church)

39.   Looking in the opposite direction from the east end of Leman Street station site on 16th May 1959, we see Brush Type 2 A1A-A1A locomotive No. D5501 heading towards Commercial Road with a freight train. Christian Street Junction signal box, which was recorded as having forty levers in 1919, formerly stood on the up side, but was abolished during the 1935 resignalling. (F. Church)

COMMERCIAL ROAD

40.   In 1881, the LTSR entered into a joint
project with the East & West India Dock
Company to construct a dock at Tilbury. So that
the anticipated traffic could be accommodated
in London, they decided to build a goods depot
at Commercial Road, which would include
warehousing for the use of the E&WIDC.
Work started in 1884, and it opened in
1886, although the dock company did not
take possession of the unfinished warehouses
until the following year. Unfortunately, the
huge development was not the success it
was hoped to be, but nevertheless the depot
remained in use until 1967. During World
War II, its deep basement provided refuge
for thousands during the Blitz, and became
known locally as 'The Tilbury Shelter'. In
1942, the warehouse received a new flat
roof after the original was damaged in an
air-raid. Our view dates from around 1905,
and shows the huge bulk of the main building,
which was erected by the contractors, J.
Mowlem & Co. To our right we see Gowers
Walk, which paralleled the depot from
Hooper Street to its entrance in Commercial
Road. (Museum of London PLA Collection)

41.   In 1903, the LTSR introduced a class of 0-6-2Ts, which eventually totalled fourteen, for working freight traffic. This is No.2186 at Commercial Road on 12th July 1913 after being taken over by the Midland Railway, and repainted in her new owner's livery. She was built by the North British Locomotive Company in 1908, and originally carried the name *Canvey Island* (K. Nunn / LCGB)

42.   We now move to 1959, and see the tracks leading to Commercial Road in diesel days, with Brush Type 2 A1A-A1A locomotive No. D5501 waiting to depart. The depot was largely demolished towards the end of 1975, so that part of the site could be redeveloped by the National Westminster Bank. By 1998, the only tangible relics comprised a hydraulic accumulator tower in Hooper Street, and a stretch of abandoned viaduct which ends abruptly at the east side of Back Church Lane. (F. Church)

CABLE STREET COAL DEPOT

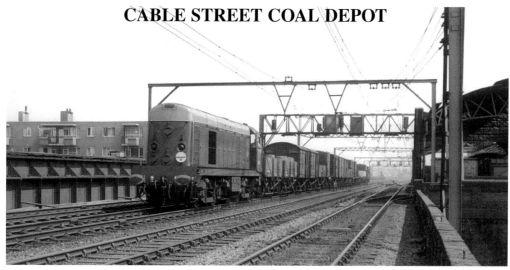

43. Looking east from near Christian Street Junction on 16th May 1959, we see English Electric Type 1 Bo-Bo diesel locomotive No. D8009 approaching with an up freight train. Just visible to the right is the roof of Cable Street coal depot, which was leased to Charrington & Co. (F. Church)

44. The depot lay on the north side of Cable Street, and stretched from Grove Street in the west to Cannon Street Road in the east. The facilities included three wagon traversers, which were supplied in 1893 by the firm of Ransomes Rapier at a cost of £200. Here we are looking from the west end in 1954. (British Rail)

45. We move on to the station at Shadwell & St. George's East station, with this very rare view looking towards Fenchurch Street in October 1949. (A.G. Ellis Collection)

SHADWELL & ST.GEORGE'S EAST

Shadwell station was opened on 1st October 1840 by the London & Blackwall Railway, and subsequently underwent various alterations. One of the most significant of these was the construction of a subway interchange with the East London Railway in 1876. The station was last rebuilt in 1895 when the formation was widened to four tracks, and the covered way leading to the ELR was improved at the same time. Its name was expanded to Shadwell & St. George's East in July 1900, and it closed on 7th July 1941. In common with Leman Street it had platforms serving the slow lines only, and was out of use for a period during World War I.

46. This is main station entrance, as it appeared in the early 1980s. It was located near the corner of Sutton Street and Shadwell Place, and is believed to date from the 1895 widening. As late as 1998 it was still possible to see cleaner patches of brickwork where the poster boards were once located, together with the remains of a gaslamp bracket, and what appeared to be the base of a signal post. (B.J. Butler)

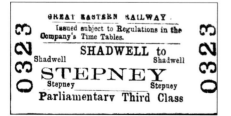

47. Because of the inter-connecting subway, it was possible to buy GER or LNER tickets at the East London Railway station in Watney Street, and ELR tickets from Shadwell & St. George's East. Here we see a doorway beneath the Blackwall viaduct in Chapman Street, which once provided side access to the ELR booking office. (V. Mitchell)

48. In August 1987, the initial sections of the Docklands Light Railway were opened to the public. This is the DLR station at Shadwell, looking west. It consists of a single island, and partially occupies the site of Shadwell & St. George's East. The platform buildings at the earlier station were stripped of their canopies in 1950, and completely demolished about five years later, leaving just a capped stairwell on the up side. (B.J. Butler)

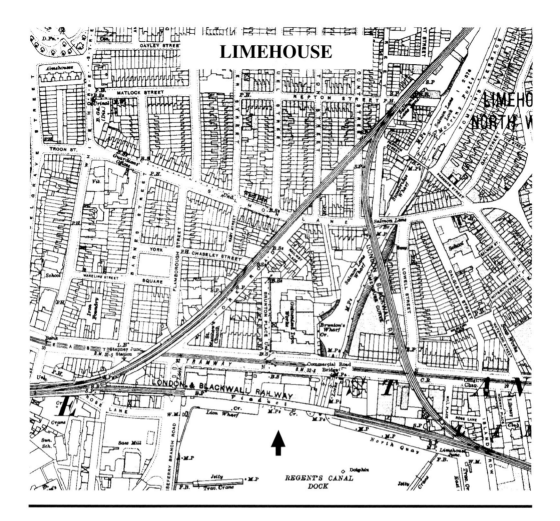

LIMEHOUSE

Here we see the Ordnance Survey Plan of 1913, showing the railway triangle north of Regents Canal Dock. The station now known as Limehouse, was originally named Stepney, and opened in August 1840. At this time, only the line running from west to east at the base of the map was in existence, as the others were later additions. Stepney station was located at the junction of the Blackwall and Blackwall Extension lines, and had platforms on all four tracks. For some reason it is indicated on the map as 'Stepney Junction', but this was never the official name. The Blackwall Extension Railway is shown curving northwards to the left of the map, and this is the route which we will be following. The other side of the triangle, seen to the right, was generally referred to as the 'Limehouse Curve', and although this was primarily intended for freight traffic, it was also used by passenger trains for two short periods in its early years.

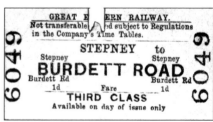

49. This is Stepney station in the 1930s, with the tracks to Bow on the left, and the Blackwall branch to the right. Behind the signal box stands a tall brick building, which was constructed as a look-out tower for signalmen controlling movements over the junction in its early days. (London Borough of Tower Hamlets)

50. From the north end of the Blackwall Extension line platforms we see LTSR 4-4-2T No.15 *East Ham* arriving with a train for Fenchurch Street. The roof on the right belongs to St. Matthews Church, which once stood near the junction of Commercial Road, and what is now Yorkshire Road. (K. Nunn / LCGB)

51.   The Blackwall branch platforms were largely demolished around 1936, leaving just a few minor traces at the London end. In this view we are looking east in the 1940s, and although colour-light signalling has been installed on the passenger lines, the overhead electrification was yet to materialise. (Lens of Sutton)

52.   The station was renamed Stepney East in 1923, but the signal box was known as Stepney Junction until after World War II. The junction itself was severed in 1951, and the track adjoining Regents Canal Dock became down-graded to a siding which was reached from the opposite end. It was finally abandoned in 1966, but the formation was later incorporated into the Docklands Light Railway. Here we see BR Standard Class 4MT 2-6-4T No.80096 about to leave Stepney East for Fenchurch Street on 21st March 1959. (F. Church)

53. Looking in the opposite direction we see a class 4MT 2-6-4T approaching with a down train. The signal box was retained during the 1930s resignalling, and suitably modernised. However its duties were replaced by a new push-button panel at Fenchurch Street during the LTS line electrification scheme, and it was finally demolished in 1961. (F. Church)

54. Stepney East station had no street level building, but was accessed by means of doorways beneath the Commercial Road bridge. At one time there was a separate entrance and exit on the south side, but these were rationalised in the 1920s following the installation of a passimeter office. This was located centrally between two barriers, and allowed the clerk to both issue and collect tickets. It survived into the 1980s, and our view shows it in its final days. (J.E. Connor)

55. Standing on the down platform in 1981, we look north-east, and see the heavy girders which formed part of the bridge over Commercial Road. The original structure of 1849 was replaced during 1874-1876 resulting in the platforms being temporarily closed for a while. It was again rebuilt during December 1995 and January 1996, when the length of the up side canopy was reduced to just the section seen in the right foreground. (J.E. Connor)

56. In anticipation of the DLR station opening on the old Blackwall formation, Stepney East was officially renamed Limehouse on 11th May 1987, although the new signs were already in position some days earlier. Here we see a pile of discarded BR platform lights incorporating the old name, lying in a corner of the booking hall prior to their removal from site. Another modification of this period was the resiting of the entrance around the corner in Bekesbourne Street to allow an easier interchange with the DLR. The doorways leading from Commercial Road have been bricked-up, and cosmetically covered with false doors. (J.E. Connor)

SALMONS LANE JUNCTION

57. Here we have a view taken from a Railway Enthusiasts' Club special on 26th August 1961, which was hauled by Ivatt class 2MT 2-6-0 No. 46472. We are waiting on the Limehouse Curve for class 4MT 2-6-4T No. 42522 to pass with the 4.40pm train from Shoeburyness to Fenchurch Street. The Limehouse Curve was opened to freight traffic on 5th April 1880, with passenger services following in September the same year. These operated between Blackwall and Palace Gates, but were clearly unsuccessful, as they were withdrawn from 1st March 1881. During 1890, the route was used by Summer excursions travelling from Blackwall to Southend, but once again these proved short lived, and ceased operating

after 1891. The curve joined the Blackwall Extension Railway 24 chains east of Stepney, at a spot known as Salmons Lane Junction, and there was a box here until the Fenchurch Street resignalling scheme of the 1930s. The line continued to be used by freight trains until 5th November 1962, and the points at Salmons Lane Junction were removed in the following May. During 1997 a very short section of viaduct was removed at the north end, therefore severing the curve from the LTS main line. Apart from this however, the entire formation was still in place in 1998, and the impressive, but disused lattice girder bridge over Commercial Road received a new coat of paint from the local council! (B.P. Pask)

London Tilbury & Southend Railway.

BURDETT ROAD to

Plaistow

GREAT EASTERN RAILWAY.

ON MONDAY, SEPTEMBER 11th, 1871,

THE

BURDETT ROAD STATION

Situate between Stepney and Bow, on the Blackwall Extension
Line, will be

OPENED

FOR

PASSENGER TRAFFIC

The FENCHURCH STREET and BOW TRAINS will call at
BURDETT ROAD STATION

EVERY QUARTER OF AN HOUR,

AS UNDER:

TO FENCHURCH ST., SHADWELL, & STEPNEY

EVERY QUARTER OF AN HOUR,

From 7.33 a.m. to 10.33 p.m. on WEEK DAYS.
From 8.3 a.m. to 11.3 a.m., and 1.3 p.m. to
10.33 p.m. on SUNDAYS.

TO BOW AND NORTH LONDON STATIONS

EVERY QUARTER OF AN HOUR,

From 7.53 a.m. to 10.38 p.m. on WEEK DAYS.
From 8.23 a.m. to 11.8 a.m., and 1.8 p.m. to
10.38 p.m. on SUNDAYS.

FARES: Burdett Road and Fenchurch Street ---

1st Class.	2nd Class.	3rd Class.		1st Class.	2nd Class.	3rd Class.
Single 8d.	4d.	3d.	Return	9d.	6d.	4d.

London, September 4th, 1871.   S. SWARBRICK, General Manager.

PRINTED AT THE COMPANY'S WORKS, STRATFORD.

BURDETT ROAD

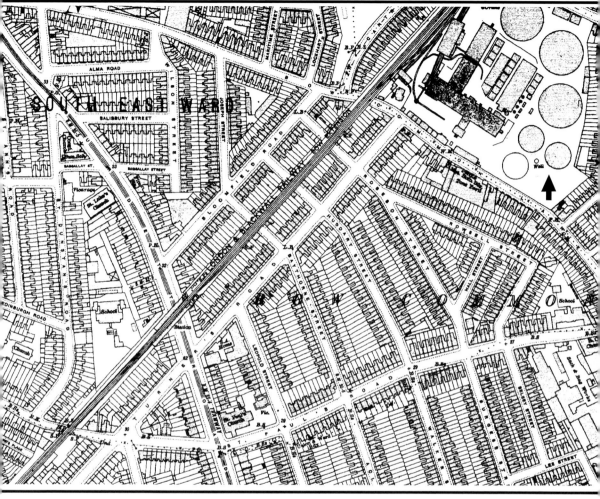

The station opened on 11th September 1871, and was situated on viaduct, 26 chains east of Stepney. It was initially served by Great Eastern services only, but from 1st November 1891 LTSR trains began to call as well. The road itself was built in 1862, and took its name from the eccentric heiress, Angela Burdett-Coutts, who spent a vast amount of her fortune on philanthropic construction schemes in the East End. Her most ambitious project was a huge, gothic styled covered market in Columbia Road, Bethnal Green, which was completed in 1869, at a cost of around £200,000. Unfortunately, despite its grandiosity, Columbia Market was a financial disaster, and lay empty and unwanted for many years before demolition.

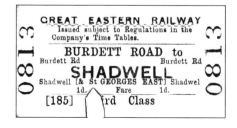

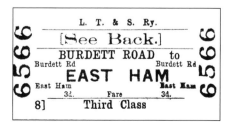

58. Like so much of the East End, the station suffered dreadfully at the hands of the Luftwaffe during the Blitz. It was hit in December 1940, and closed for about a week whilst emergency repairs were carried out. It then reopened, but closed again after the raid of 10th April 1941, and never brought back into use. Here we are looking north along Burdett Road soon after the second attack, and see that the wooden rear wall of the up platform has gone, along with the canopy it once supported. Unfortunately, the photograph is far from sharp, but it appears that the surviving section of valancing on the down side was of a type different to that employed elsewhere on the line. (London Borough of Tower Hamlets)

59. Approval to demolish the remaining platform buildings came in October 1950, and no time was lost in pulling them down. This view, taken from a train heading towards Gas Factory Junction, shows the up side around 1951, and judging from the rubble lying around, the demolition men appear to have not long departed. The platforms themselves lingered on for a few more years, but had gone by the early 1960s. (Photographer unknown : J.E. Connor Collection)

60. As with Stepney station, Burdett Road had no street level building. Instead, there was a pedestrian archway on the east side of the thoroughfare, which led to the entrance. Here we are looking south towards the Blitz-scarred arch in 1969. (J.E. Connor)

GREAT EASTERN RAILWAY
Issued subject to Regulations in the
Company's Time Tables.
BURDETT ROAD to
Burdett Rd   Burdett Rd
FENCHURCH ST
Fenchurch St   Fenchurch St
2d.   Fare   2d.
669   Third Class

5851   5851

61. Inside the arch we see the former street level entrance in 1984, shortly before it disappeared during road widening. For many years it was used as a woodworking factory, and had timber stacked on its surviving sections of stairway. (J.E. Connor)

GAS FACTORY JUNCTION

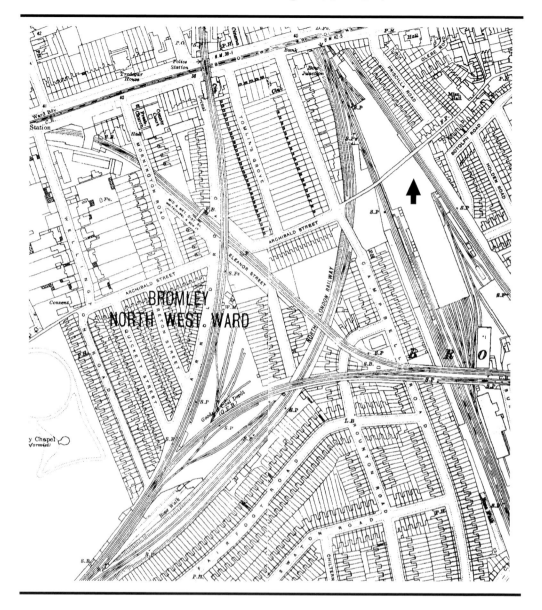

In this Ordnance Survey map of 1913, we see Gas Factory Junction at the bottom left, with the original North London route of 1850 veering off on the right, then curving northwards. Above this, the London Tilbury & Southend main line parts company with the Blackwall Extension Railway and heads east. Close to the junction, lies Bow Road goods depot, which was opened by the GER around 1885 and closed in 1964. After passing over the curve onto the NLR, the LTS reached Campbell Road Junction, where the Whitechapel & Bow Joint Railway can be see coming in from the north-west. A little to the east of Campbell Road, the LTS was carried above the North London Poplar branch on a lattice girder bridge, and passengers could gain a fleeting glimpse of the vast NLR Bow Works complex which lay beneath them in a wide cutting.

62. On 13th June 1959 we see English Electric Type 1 Bo-Bo diesel locomotive No. D8014 from Devons Road shed, crossing onto the Gas Factory Junction-Bow spur with a freight for the North London line. The plate displaying '2' carried by the loco denotes its duty number. (F. Church)

63. Looking in the opposite direction on the same day, we witness Stanier 3-cylinder class 4MT 2-6-4T No.42509 bringing an up train past the signal box. The track immediately to the right of the locomotive descended to Bow Road goods depot, whilst the adjoining line was part of the spur onto the North London. (F. Church)

64. BR Standard Class 4MT 2-6-4T No. 80075 approaches with an up train, having just passed over the junction with the electrified Blackwall Extension line on 13th June 1959. The tracks of the spur onto the North London can be seen in the foreground, but the line leading to Bow Road Goods is hidden by the wall. (F. Church)

←

65. The signal box was retained during the Fenchurch Street resignalling of the mid-1930s, but equipped with a new panel. Prior to conversion it contained fifty-one working levers and three spare. Automatic signalling was introduced between Gas Factory Junction and Upminster as part of the LTS electrification scheme, and the box became redundant. Here it is seen from a passing train in 1959. (Photographer unknown/J.E. Connor Collection)

66. In this view, we are looking west, as BR Standard class 4MT 2-6-4T No. 80104 leaves the Blackwall Extension line and runs onto former LTS metals with a fast Fenchurch Street-Southend train. To the left is a section of Bow gasworks, whilst to the right are the tracks to Stratford. (F. Church)

67. Bow Road goods depot was located at a lower level than the passenger lines. Here, BR Standard class 4MT 2-6-4T No. 80131 passes some of the sidings on 18th May 1959, as she works a down train from Fenchurch Street. The main part of the depot was situated between the LTS line, and the Blackwall Extension route, which is seen diverging to the right of the locomotive. (F. Church)

CAMPBELL ROAD JUNCTION

DISTRICT RAILWAY.

G.O. 9.

NOTICE TO STAFF

RESPECTING

OPENING OF WHITECHAPEL & BOW JOINT LINE.

1. *The Extension from WHITECHAPEL to BROMLEY (L. T. & S. Railway) will be opened for Public Traffic on Monday, 2nd June, 1902, from which date Whitechapel Station will be re-opened and must be considered as a Station on Whitechapel and Bow Joint Line.*

2. The names of the Stations are :—

WHITECHAPEL (for Bethnal Green Museum, Cambridge Heath, East London Railway, London Hospital, Mile End Gate, &c.)

STEPNEY GREEN (for Beaumont Hall, Devonshire Street, Globe Road, People's Palace, Stepney Green, White Horse Lane, &c.)

MILE END (for Bow Common, Burdett Road, People's Palace, Tower Hamlets Cemetery, Victoria Park, &c.)

BOW ROAD (for Bow and Bromley Institute, Bow County Court, Bow Vestry Hall, Campbell Road, Old Ford, &c.)

3. The Station Initials are :—

WHITECHAPEL
STEPNEY GREEN
MILE END
BOW ROAD

4. The Junction between Bow Joint Line and Tilbury Railway is situated about midway between Bow Road and Bromley Stations, and will be known as Campbell Road Junction.

NOTE.—Stepney Green and Bow Road will not be opened for public traffic on 2nd June, and therefore until further notice the Trains for Passenger purposes will run from Whitechapel to Mile End and from Mile End to Bromley and *vice versa*.

5. The Train Service over Bow Joint Line will be formed by projecting Whitechapel Trains (supplemented by others from District system) on to Bow Road, where some of the Trains will terminate, the others running through to

BROMLEY,	UPTON PARK
WEST HAM,	AND
PLAISTOW,	EAST HAM.

With a few exceptions (for which see Time Tables), the regular Train Service will terminate at East Ham.

N.B.—Bromley Station is "BROMLEY-BY-BOW," and must not be confused with Bromley (Kent), which is served by Stations on S.E. & C. Railway.

68. On 18th August 1959, we see a District Line train taking the junction, and heading west onto the former Whitechapel & Bow Joint Railway. The signal box was opened in 1905 as part of the Campbell Road-East Ham quadrupling scheme, and replaced a short-lived 1902 cabin which stood a little further east. (F. Church)

69. We are now looking in the opposite direction, as BR Standard Class 4MT 2-6-4T approaches the junction on 18th May 1959. The District Line tracks are just out of sight, to the right of the signal box. (F. Church)

70. A little to the east of Campbell Road, the line is carried above the former North London Railway on an impressive girder bridge. This replaced an earlier structure in 1904, and is seen on 18th May 1959, with Stanier three-cylinder class 4MT 2-6-4T No. 42502 working a down fast train. (F. Church)

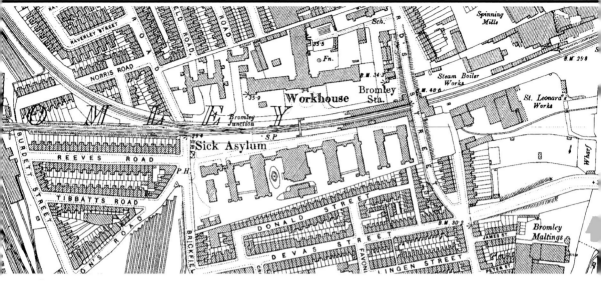

The original Bromley station of 1858 comprised two platforms, and stood on the east side of St. Leonards Street. It was badly damaged by fire in December 1892, and subsequently resited to the west. The new station, which opened on 1st March 1894, as a direct replacement for its predecessor is shown on the 1895 Ordnance Survey map above. It is interesting to note, that although the bulk of the premises had been moved to the opposite side of the road, the new street level building occupied the original site, and was connected to the platforms by means of a subway. To the west of the station can be seen the double track connection from the NLR, whilst to the north lies the dreaded workhouse, one of the less savoury aspects of 19th century London.

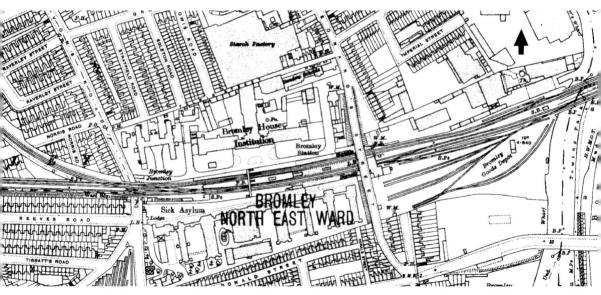

We now see the station in 1914 after quadrupling, and the addition of a goods yard to the east of St. Leonards Street. On the right is the River Lea.

71. Looking west from an up train on 27th September 1958 we see the junction of the Bromley-Bow curve, which opened in May 1869. When constructed, the two North London tracks paralleled the LTSR almost to St. Leonards Street, but when Bromley station was resited, the junction had to be moved as well. It was a useful connection, and in its day hosted through services between the NLR and Thames Estuary destinations such as Tilbury and Southend. The spur was also used by local North London trains which shuttled back and forth between Bow and Plaistow, but these ceased from 1st January 1916. These workings were never restored, but between 1923 and 1935, the curve was used by certain LTS line trains which ran into Broad Street to alleviate congestion at Fenchurch Street. The Bromley-Bow connection continued to be used by excursion traffic after World War II, but it was finally closed in 1959 and subsequently lifted. (F. Church)

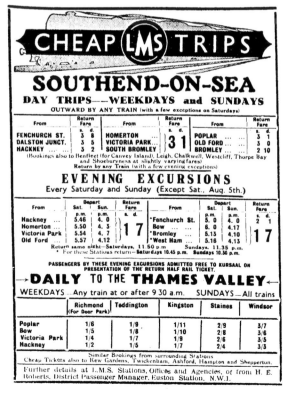

CHEAP LMS TRIPS

SOUTHEND-ON-SEA

DAY TRIPS—WEEKDAYS and SUNDAYS

OUTWARD BY ANY TRAIN (with a few exceptions on Saturdays)

From	Return Fare	From	Return Fare	From	Return Fare
	s. d.				s. d.
FENCHURCH ST.	3 8	HOMERTON		POPLAR	3 1
DALSTON JUNCT.	3 5	VICTORIA PARK	3 1	OLD FORD	3 0
HACKNEY	3 2	SOUTH BROMLEY		BROMLEY	2 10

(Bookings also to Benfleet (for Canvey Island), Leigh, Chalkwell, Westcliff, Thorpe Bay and Shoeburyness at slightly varying fares)
Return by any Train (with a few evening exceptions)

EVENING EXCURSIONS

Every Saturday and Sunday (Except Sat., Aug. 5th.)

From	Depart Sat.	Sun.	Return Fare	From	Depart Sat.	Sun.	Return Fare
	p.m.	p.m.	s. d.		p.m.	p.m.	s. d.
Hackney	5.46	4. 0		*Fenchurch St.	5. 0	4. 0	
Homerton	5.50	4. 5	1 7	Bow	6. 0	4.17	2 1
Victoria Park	5.54	4. 7		*Bromley	5.13	4.10	1 7
Old Ford	5.57	4.12		*West Ham	5.16	4.13	

Return same night—Saturdays, 11.50 p.m   Sundays, 11.35 p.m.
* For these Stations return—Saturdays 10.45 p.m.   Sundays 10.30 p.m.

PASSENGERS BY THESE EVENING EXCURSIONS ADMITTED FREE TO KURSAAL ON PRESENTATION OF THE RETURN HALF RAIL TICKET.

→DAILY TO THE THAMES VALLEY←

WEEKDAYS...Any train at or after 9 30 a.m.   SUNDAYS—All trains

	Richmond (For Deer Park)	Teddington	Kingston	Staines	Windsor
Poplar	1/6	1/9	1/11	2/9	3/7
Bow	1/5	1/8	1/10	2/8	3/6
Victoria Park	1/4	1/7	1/9	2/6	3/5
Hackney	1/2	1/5	1/7	2/4	3/3

Similar Bookings from surrounding Stations
Cheap Tickets also to Kew Gardens, Twickenham, Ashford, Hampton and Shepperton.

Further details at L.M.S. Stations, Offices and Agencies, or from H. E. Roberts, District Passenger Manager, Euston Station, N.W.1.

72. The curve was also used for freight traffic, as seen here on 11th September 1959 with a BTH Type 1 Bo-Bo diesel locomotive crossing the District Line tracks west of Bromley station. Judging from the fact that one or more official photographers were in attendance, this may have been the last train. (British Rail)

73. In this view from the station footbridge dated 5th December 1959, it appears that the junction had just been severed. The signal box was built in connection with the 1905 quadrupling, and replaced an earlier structure from 1893. The missing arms on the adjoining signal post bear witness to the recently abandoned crossover and curve onto the North London. The footpath to the left of the box led to an entrance in Devons Road. (Photographer unknown / J.E. Connor Collection)

74. The station was provided with an entrance in Devons Road around 1895. This proved useful for railwaymen employed at the nearby North London locomotive depot, and visitors to St. Andrews Hospital. It was closed in 1940, but reopened from 5th January 1948. The entrance was provided with a separate booking office, and connected to the up through line platform by stairs and inclined ramp. It was finally abandoned on 26th April 1970, but traces still remained in the 1990s. (J.E. Connor)

75. The main street level building stood on the east side of St. Leonards Street, and dated from the resiting of 1894. It was badly damaged by fire on 20th February 1970, and replaced by a temporary entrance in Talwin Street two months later. This sufficed until 11th June 1972 when a new permanent building was opened opposite the original site. This view shows the 1894 structure soon after closure, with the boarded-up Station Master's house to the right. (J.E. Connor)

76. Apart from LTS and District trains, Bromley was also served by GE line workings which travelled by way of the Abbey Mills spur near West Ham. This view shows class F4 2-4-2T No. 7074 standing at the station in the 1930s with a train of antiquated stock from either North Woolwich or Gallions to Fenchurch Street. When the Abbey Mills spur first opened, Great Eastern services were not permitted to call at Bromley, but began doing so in 1883. This arrangement ceased after just four years however, but was reinstated in 1891 as part of an agreement which also allowed LTSR trains to call at Burdett Road. (Stations UK)

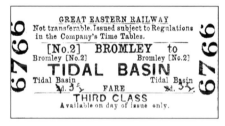

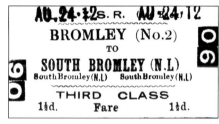

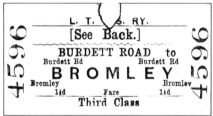

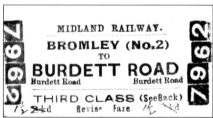

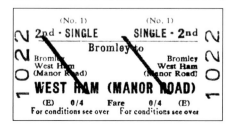

77. The crew of Jinty 0-6-0T No. 47312 look very relaxed, and smile for the camera, as they work a trip freight from Plaistow through the station on 21st July 1951. The locomotive was allocated to Devons Road depot at the time, and was regularly used on local workings around East London. (P.J. Lynch)

78. In readiness for the LTS line electrification, the footbridge at Bromley station had to be rebuilt, so that there was clearance for the overhead wires. Here we are looking east from the up fast line platform on 14th March 1959. (Photographer unknown / J.E. Connor Collection)

79. Looking east from the footbridge in 1965, we have a general view of the station with the District Line tracks on the left, and the BR side to the right. British Railways' services which called at Bromley were phased out, and ceased altogether with electrification, therefore the up fast line platform, and one side of the island fell into disuse. The street level building can be seen in the middle distance. (J.E. Connor)

80. The premises were renamed Bromley-By-Bow on 18th May 1967, presumably to avoid confusion with stations south of the Thames in the London Borough of Bromley. The awnings on the disused up through platform were removed around 1968, and in January the following year ownership was transferred from British Rail to London Transport. The street level building fire of 1970 hastened comprehensive rebuilding, and this was duly completed by June 1972. Here we look east along the down District Line platform, and see work in progress. (J.E. Connor)

81. On the up side of the line, east of St. Leonards Street lay the sidings of Bromley goods yard, which opened around 1898. In this 1958 view we see the sidings to the right, and a girder bridge in the middle distance, spanning the River Lea. To the left, a venerable Q23 car heads a District Line train for Wimbledon, having just passed an eastbound service. (H.C. Casserley)

82. Until the advent of the Greater London Council, the River Lea formed the boundary between London and Essex. The LTSR bridge consisted of two 190ft spans, of which the first replaced an earlier structure in 1889, whilst the second was added during the quadrupling of 1905. The small signal box was called Bromley Ground Cabin, and was opened in 1906. This view, looking east, shows BR Standard class 4MT 2-6-4T No. 80103 crossing from the Essex side with an up train on 1st May 1959. (F. Church)

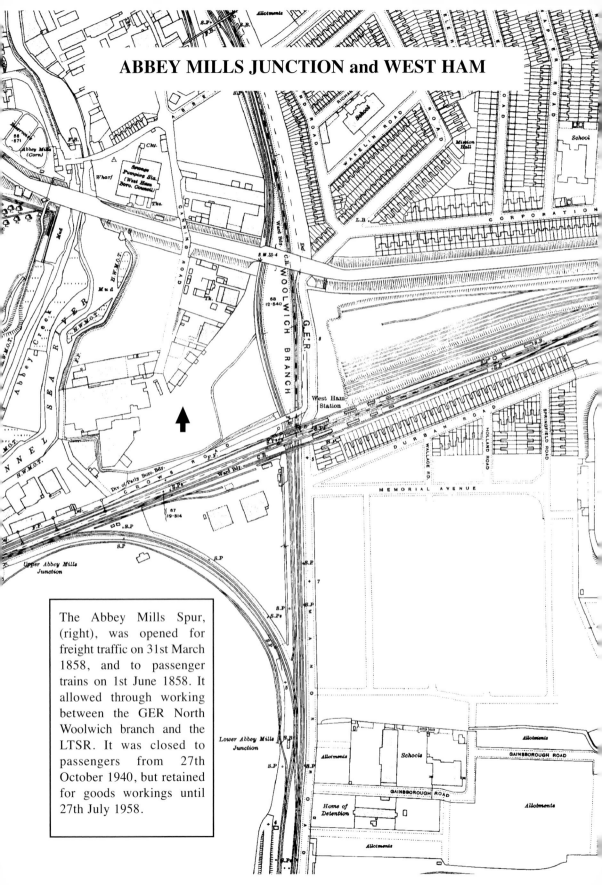

ABBEY MILLS JUNCTION and WEST HAM

The Abbey Mills Spur, (right), was opened for freight traffic on 31st March 1858, and to passenger trains on 1st June 1858. It allowed through working between the GER North Woolwich branch and the LTSR. It was closed to passengers from 27th October 1940, but retained for goods workings until 27th July 1958.

83. This is Upper Abbey Mills Junction signal box as it appeared on 1st July 1959. It was opened in 1904 to replace an earlier structure, and remained in use until 1961. After the Abbey Mills Spur was closed to all traffic in 1958, the junction with the North Woolwich branch was severed, but the majority of track was retained as a siding, accessed from the LTS line, until 7th August 1960. (F. Church)

84. West Ham station was opened on 1st February 1901, and rebuilt with two island platforms in 1905. It was renamed West Ham Manor Road by the LMSR on 11th February 1924, but otherwise remained more or less unchanged until World War II. Here we see the street level entrance in the 1970s. The fence to the left separated the pavement from the North Woolwich branch, but no station was provided here until 14th May 1979. Additional platforms were added alongside during the late 1990s to serve the Jubilee Line Extension, and by 1998 work was well advanced on combining the existing premises into a major interchange. (J.E. Connor)

85. With ex-LMSR class 3P 4-4-2T No. 41936 pounding through the rain on 17th March 1951, we have a wonderfully evocative view of an east London station in the days of steam. Regular LTSR trains ceased to call here in 1913, leaving the through platforms for the use of NLR services only. When these ceased in World War I, the southernmost island virtually fell into disuse, although it was retained for emergencies. The station was closed after 7th September 1940 due to severe local bomb damage, but when it reopened on 11th August 1941, the through platforms remained shut. By the time this photograph was taken it seems that most of the glass had gone from the stairway which once served them. (H.C. Casserley)

86. The disused island was demolished in 1956, leaving just a widening in the formation, and capped stairwell to indicated its former existence. This view, taken from a similar angle to the photograph above shows a BR Standard class 4MT 2-6-4T passing with a train from Fenchurch Street in the late 1950s. (B.P. Pask)

87. Here we have a busy scene, as an extremely grimy BR Standard Class 4MT 2-6-4T works a down service past the station in the late 1950s. A westbound District Line train is in the process of departing, as one travelling in the opposite direction arrives behind the platform building. The style of supports used on the nameboard indicates that prior to nationalisation, it was one of the 'hawkseye' type, introduced by the LMSR around 1936. In September 1997 Railtrack agreed to erect of a new platform on the site of that which was demolished in 1956 at an estimated cost of £3million. (B.P. Pask)

88. The signal box was located to the east of the island which served the District Line. It was opened in 1901, and is seen here on 1st March 1959. (F. Church)

PLAISTOW MOTIVE POWER DEPOT

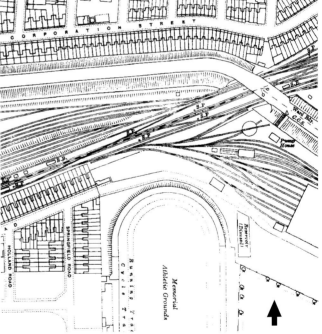

90. Here we have a general view of Plaistow MPD, looking east on 6th July 1959. The depot was opened as 'West Ham' on 30th September 1911, and was located on the up side between West Ham and Plaistow stations. Its facilites lay to the west of the Northern Outfall Sewer, as seen from the 1914 Ordnance Survey plan on the right. The original LTSR running sheds were on the opposite side of the line, at the west end of Plaistow station, but these were closed when the adjoining locomotive works were expanded. In LMSR and early BR days, the shedcode for Plaistow was '13A', but this was changed to '33A' when the LTS line was transferred to the Eastern Region. (F. Church)

89. From 1st January 1969, the ownership of all intermediate stations between Campbell Road Junction and Upminster, with the exception of Barking, was transferred from British Rail to London Transport. This made no difference to the services, as by then, no BR trains called. The new owners lost no time in removing the 'Manor Road' suffix, and replacing the earlier signs with their own distinctive roundels. This view, taken on the day of the changeover shows a BR Eastern Region totem and its replacement, shortly before the former was removed. (J.E. Connor)

91. Outside the Plaistow running sheds we can admire No. 2101, one of a class of eight 4-6-4Ts, which entered traffic in 1913. These were designed by LTSR Locomotive Superintendent Robert Harben Whitelegg, but emerged after the line had been taken over by the Midland. They weighed over 94 tons, and in their day were the heaviest passenger tank engines in the country. This fact was used by the Great Eastern to bar them from using their line west of Gas Factory Junction, so these handsome machines were never seen at Fenchurch Street. Because of the GE restriction, they virtually became 'white elephants', and were almost immediately offered for sale. In the Spring of 1913, trials were held on both the Great Western and South Eastern & Chatham, but neither company was impressed with their performance, and even though the Midland were happy to accept a bargain price, no sales materialised. During World War I, they were transferred to other parts of the system, but despite their huge bulk, their limited coal capacity meant they were unsuited to long-distance work. Scrapping commenced in 1929, and by 1934 the entire class of eight locomotives was extinct. (H.L. Hopwood / LCGB)

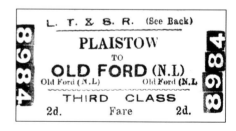

92. Being such a busy line, there was always plenty of activity to be seen around Plaistow MPD. Here Stanier 3-cylinder class 4MT 2-6-4T No.42506 hurries by with an up train for Fenchurch Street, as sister engines 42522, 42516 and 42514 prepare to come off shed. (F. Church)

93. The LTSR combined water tank and coaling stage at Plaistow was a very distinctive structure. In later years a new coaler was added alongside, and this is seen here about to replenish the bunker of BR Standard Class 4MT 2-6-4T No. 80077 on 6th August 1959. (F. Church)

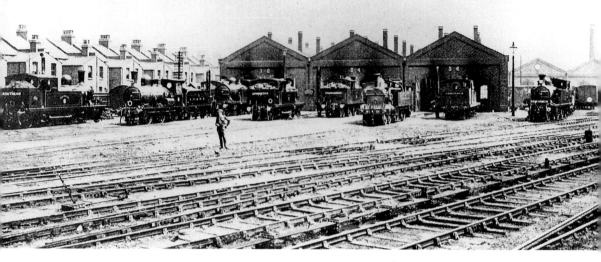

94. As mentioned earlier, the original running shed was much closer to Plaistow station. In this view we see a variety of motive power, including an LTSR 0-6-0 goods engine, and a Metropolitan District Railway 4-4-0T, which has worked in over the Whitechapel & Bow line. According to a handwritten note on the original photograph, the gentleman standing in front of the yard is Mr. R. H. Whitelegg, whilst just visible on the extreme right is a section of the works. (Photographer unknown / J.E. Connor Collection)

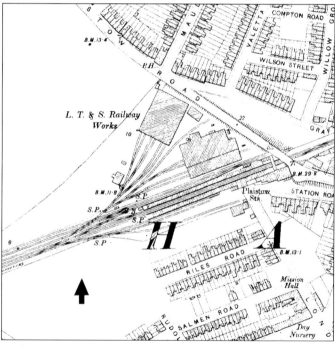

The shed adjoined the western end of the workshops, but as it was not opened until 1899, it does not appear on the 1894 OS plan. What is shown however is the complex of buildings and tracks dating from 1879-80, which served the line into early LMSR days. The locomotive works closed in 1925, when the responsibility of maintenance was transferred to Bow on the former North London Railway, but the Carriage & Wagon department lingered on until 1932, when the work was relocated to Wolverton, together with a number of staff. After closure, the buildings were adapted for non-railway use.

PLAISTOW

95. Looking east towards Plaistow station on 1st March 1959 we see part of the former works, which for a number of years was leased to the German car manufacturer Volkswagen. A District Line train, led by a Q23 type car has just departed from the down side bay, and is heading towards central London. The signal box seen on the right was opened in 1903 whilst quadrupling was in progress, and replaced a box which dated from 1880. It was rendered redundant on the run up to electrification, and demolished in 1961. (F. Church)

96. We now move to the central island, and look at the station, as it appeared in the 1930s. At this time there were six platform faces, of which the outer pair were bays. The down bay is on the extreme left, and a train of clerestory roof District Line stock can just be seen beneath the canopy. Adjoining this are the two tracks used by Underground services, whilst to the right are the LTS through lines. Beyond these is the up side bay, which was provided in 1905 for the North London Railway Bow service, but closed to regular passenger traffic following their withdrawal during World War I. (Stations UK)

97. The clerestory roof Q Stock was a familiar sight on the District Line, until the vehicles were withdrawn in the early 1970s. Here an eastbound service stands at Plaistow station in 1968, with a Q23 car nearest the camera. (I. Baker)

98. The street level building stands on the west side of Plaistow High Street, and dates from 1882. When opened, the original station entrance led directly onto the up platform, and passengers wishing to travel in the opposite direction had to cross the line on the level, as no footbridge or subway was provided. This view dates from 1969, soon after ownership was transferred to London Transport, and although a British Railways totem can still be see to the right, the sign above the entrance displays a pair of LT roundels, with no mention of BR. The building still survived in 1998, although the ornate balustrading around the top had sadly disappeared. (I. Baker)

UPTON PARK

99. The station was built to serve new residential housing in the area, and opened in September 1877. It was constructed by a local developer, who felt that its existence would be a selling point for his houses, so the only expense incurred by the LTSR was a contribution of £400. Here we are looking northwards along Green Street, in the early years of the twentieth century, with the street level building to the left, on the corner of Queen's Square. Upton Park station was completely rebuilt during the widening, and none of the earlier structures were retained. (Commercial Postcard / J.E. Connor Collection)

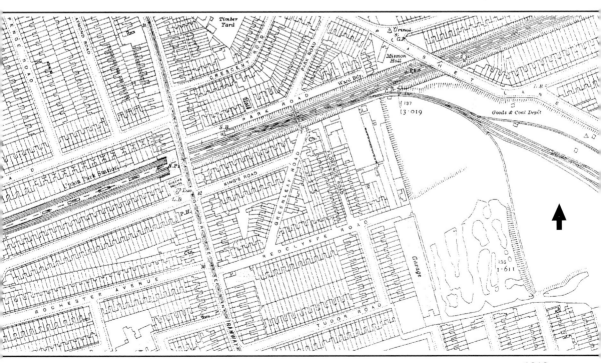

1919

100. The street level building constructed for the widening was much larger and more spacious than its predecessor. Here we see it on a busy Saturday morning in 1989. (J.E. Connor)

101. About three decades earlier, we look eastwards along the platform, and see a District Line train for Ealing Broadway arriving. The rebuilding of the station was completed during 1903 and 1904. (Stations UK)

102. From the footbridge linking Park Road and Kings Road, we look back towards the station on 10th August 1958, as British Railways Standard Class 4MT 2-6-4T No.80135 approaches with a down train. Upton Park signal box, seen to the right was opened in May 1904, and closed in 1961. (F. Church)

103. Looking in the opposite direction we observe 'Jinty' 0-6-0T No.47484 approaching with an up freight train. The junction to the right of the locomotive led to Upton Park goods and coal depot, which was opened by the London & North Western Railway on 1st April 1895. This occupied the site of an earlier LNWR ballast siding, which only lasted from 1874 until the following decade when it was lifted. The depot had a much longer life however, and survived until July 1989. (F. Church)

EAST HAM

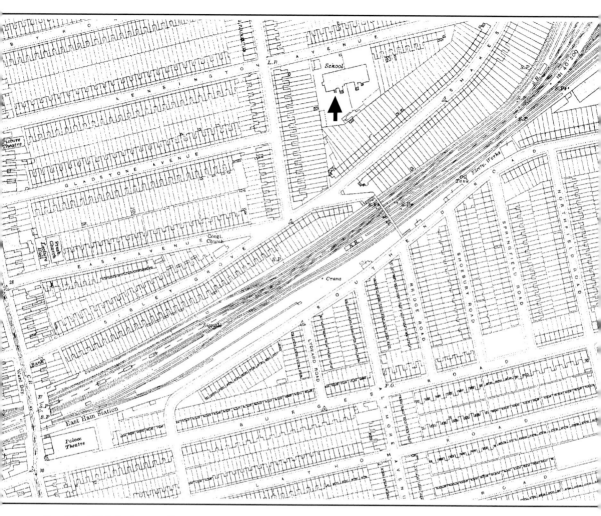

On this 1920 Ordnance Survey map, the station is shown to the left, with its goods yard and East Ham No.2 signal box near the centre. To the right are Little Ilford Carriage sidings, together with Little Ilford No.1 signal box. This stood near the junction of a spur used by services onto the Tottenham & Forest Gate Line from 1894 until 1958.

London Tilbury & Southend Railway.

Burdett Road
TO
East Ham

104. Looking east from the High Street bridge in the late 1880s, we can note that the surrounding area was still largely rural. When opened in 1858, the premises were extremely sparse, and remained so until a new main building was erected on the up platform, a few years before this photograph was taken. (Lens of Sutton)

105. This view shows the building on the down side, after receiving roof damage. Unfortunately the original print is undated, and bears no information as to the cause. With the advent of the Tottenham & Forest Gate line in 1894, the platforms at East Ham were lengthened from 380ft to 560ft, and a bay provided on the down side. At the same time a lattice iron footbridge was added near the country end to improve interchange facilities between the new TFGR and the existing up platform. (J.E. Connor Collection)

106. The street level building at East Ham was erected in 1903-4. It has undergone comparatively few changes throughout its existence, and was still in use in 1998. (J.E. Connor)

107. Pictured on 16th August 1958 is 'Jinty' 0-6-0T No.47484 running light on the down through line. During rebuilding, the original platforms were retained, although the up side was converted to an island. New buildings and canopies were provided, and the station's appearance was completely transformed. The bay used by TFGR trains remained as before, although the redevelopment resulted in it being shortened slightly. This can be seen to the extreme right, with a train for Kentish Town, hauled by a Stanier class 3MT 2-6-2T awaiting to leave. To the left we have the up through line platform, which was a completely new addition when built in 1904. (H.C. Casserley)

108. The tracks used by BR trains were slightly realigned in 1959 so that a new headshunt serving a carriage washer could be laid between them. This meant that the up through platform had to be resited a little further south than its predecessor. Here it is seen with class 4MT 2-6-4T No. 42528 passing on her way to Fenchurch Street. The new platform served little purpose, as it was scarcely used, and officially closed in 1962. It was still standing in 1998, although its coping and lamps had long-since been removed. (F. Church).

109. Looking west from Jews Farm footbridge on 16th May 1958, we can examine the good yard which was added at the time of quadrupling. At first there were no freight facilities at East Ham, but in 1889 a pair of sidings were brought into use at the London end of the station. The more recent establishment seen here was connected to the main line at both ends, and was accessed through a gate on the north side of Southend Road. The signal box is East Ham No.2. This opened in May 1904, together with East Ham No.1, which was west of the High Street bridge. In the background a Kentish Town train is departing. This service was withdrawn from 15th September 1958, and the track into the bay was subsequently lifted. (F. Church)

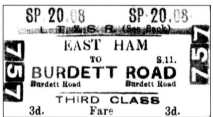

110. Still at the Jews Lane footbridge, we look east, as Stanier class 4MT 2-6-4T makes a smoky departure from Little Ilford carriage sidings with an empty stock working. The signal box visible to the left is Little Ilford No. 1. (F. Church)

111. We now stand beside the line at Little Ilford No.1, and see the tail end of a westbound District Line train heading towards East Ham station. Just visible in the distance is the Jews Lane footbridge which provided our viewpoint for the previous two photographs. The signal box dated from 1908, and replaced an earlier structure which was sited slightly to its south-west. (F. Church)

Just beyond Little Ilford No.1 signal box, the 'Loop Line' used by TFGR trains diverged northwards. On this Ordnance Survey map of 1894, we can see that there were very few buildings nearby, and that the district remained almost completely rural. On 20th August 1905 a number of sidings for MDR electric stock were brought into use adjoining the main line, and within a few years these evolved into Little Ilford depot. Nearby lay the nine roads of Little Ilford Southern Carriage Sidings, which were opened by the LTSR in 1908. In time, the small MDR shed and its attendant stabling facilities became inadequate, so it was replaced by a much larger District Line depot at Upminster, which opened on 1st December 1958.

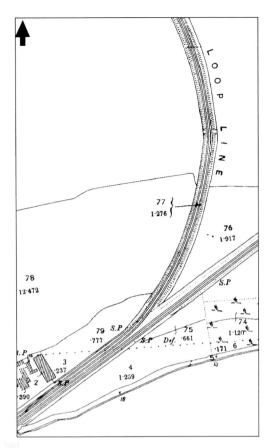

112. The demise of the London Transport facilities at Little Ilford was also hastened by LTS line electrification, and the need for new BR car sheds. These subsequently became known as East Ham depot, and are seen here under construction, as British Railways Standard class 4MT 2-6-4T No.80076 passes with an up train. (F. Church)

1894

114. A further rebuilding came when the line between Little Ilford and Barking was quadrupled between 1906 and 1908. As part of this scheme, the East Street level crossing was removed, and replaced by a bridge, from which a new street level building provided access to the station. Here we look towards the frontage on 26th November 1957, as an SA3 type trolleybus approaches on route 693 to Chadwell Heath. These vehicles were originally intended for export to Johannesburg, but the onset of World War II, and the threat of U-Boat attacks on British shipping resulted in them staying in England. Together with classes SA1 and SA2, which were built for service in Durban, they were the first 8ft. wide vehicles in the LT fleet, and special permission had to be given before they entered service on account of their extra width. (F. Church)

113. Barking was one of the original stations on the LTSR, and opened with the line on 13th April 1854. Originally it served a fishing village, but with the advent of the railway the surrounding area began to develop. In this view we are looking west over the East Street level crossing, sometime in the late nineteenth or early twentieth century, and see a station which had already undergone substantial alterations. The most notable of these took place during 1889, when a down loop and up bay were added. (J.E. Connor Collection)

115. The rebuilding of 1906-8 resulted in the station having eight platform faces, of which Nos. 4 and 5 were bays for the MDR electric services. In 1911 the tracks into platforms 2 and 3 were also electrified, and amongst the trains which used these were the through workings between Ealing Broadway and Southend. Here we see one of these services, formed of corridor stock arriving at platform 2. It is hauled by a pair of Metropolitan District Railway electric locomotives, and carries a headboard stating *Southend Corridor Express*. On arrival, the engines would be detached, and the train would continue to its destination behind steam. The box-like MDR electric locos belonged to a class of ten, which were built by the Metropolitan Amalgamated Railway Carriage & Wagon Company in 1905. They were originally used to haul LNWR Outer Circle trains on the section between Earls Court and Mansion House, but were rendered redundant when the service was cut back to Earls Court in 1909. Three of them were scrapped soon afterwards, but the remainder survived, and were later used between Ealing and Barking. They were not the most powerful of machines, and generally worked in pairs as can be seen here. (K. Nunn / LCGB)

North London Railway

TO

BARKING

116. Here we see the station in the 1930s, looking east from a signal gantry which once spanned the tracks at the London end. On our right, class 4MT 2-6-4T No.2534 awaits departure for Fenchurch Street, whilst to the far left a District Line service stands at platform 3. Next to this at No.4 is a train of F Stock, which carries a destination board for Hounslow. F Stock dated from 1920, and was often referred to by the nickname of *Tanks*. These units were constructed for the MDR, but latterly saw service on the Metropolitan and East London Lines. The last sets were withdrawn in 1963, and none have been preserved. (Real Photographs)

117. Further rebuilding came in the late 1950s, when the track layout was altered to improve traffic flow prior to electrification. In connection with this, two flyovers were constructed at the west end. and a dive-under was added to the east. Here, Type 2 diesel No D6112 is seen passing a District Line train formed of COP stock on 22nd August 1960, as she climbs towards the flyover with a rake of empty coaches. (F. Church)

118. BR Standard class 4MT 2-6-4T No.80071 runs alongside platform 6 on 28th February 1959, with the 11.40am train from Fenchurch Street to Tilbury. The signal box visible in the background is Barking West, which replaced the old Barking Yard box in the early part of 1908. (H.C. Casserley)

119. Looking from the London end a few months later on 6th June, we see that the track alongside platform 6 has been removed. This had previously been the down main, but thanks to the existence of the new dive-under, it was about to become the westbound District. When rebuilding had been completed, platform 1 was allocated to trains serving Kentish Town (now Gospel Oak), platform 2 was for the eastbound District Line, and a bay, No 3, was for Underground terminators. Down and up Shoeburyness workings called at numbers 4 and 5 respectively, whilst the westbound District used No 6, as mentioned above. The remaining faces, numbers 7 and 8, were for down and up trains serving the route via Tilbury. (Photographer unknown / J.E. Connor Collection)

120. This is the interior of the booking hall, after station rebuilding had been completed. Its official opening took place on 29th September 1961, when the Mayor of Barking unveiled a commemorative plaque within the concourse area. The impressive new premises were constructed on the site of the 1908 street level building, so temporary offices had to be provided between the demolition of one, and erection of the other. The high roof was fabricated from precast concrete members, and featured cranked cantilever beams, capped at the ends by concrete valance units. These had a span of 48ft., and projected 18ft. beyond the concourse to form an exterior canopy sheltering a new lay-by. (Stations UK)

London Tilbury & Southend Railway.

BURDETT ROAD to

Barking

MP Middleton Press

Easebourne Lane, Midhurst, West Sussex. GU29 9AZ Tel: 01730 813169 Fax: 01730 812601

If books are not available from you local transport stockist, order direct with cheque, Visa or Mastercard, post free UK.

BRANCH LINES
Branch Line to Allhallows
Branch Lines to Alton
Branch Lines around Ascot
Branch Line to Ashburton
Branch Lines around Bodmin
Branch Line to Bude
Branch Lines around Canterbury
Branch Line to Cheddar
Branch Lines to East Grinstead
Branch Lines to Effingham Junction
Branch Line to Fairford
Branch Line to Hawkhurst
Branch Line to Hayling
Branch Lines to Horsham
Branch Line to Ilfracombe
Branch Line to Kingswear
Branch Lines to Launceston & Princetown
Branch Lines to Longmoor
Branch Line to Looe
Branch Line to Lyme Regis
Branch Lines around Midhurst
Branch Line to Minehead
Branch Line to Newport (IOW)
Branch Line to Padstow
Branch Lines around Plymouth
Branch Lines to Seaton & Sidmouth
Branch Line to Selsey
Branch Lines around Sheerness
Branch Line to Tenterden
Branch Lines to Torrington
Branch Lines to Tunbridge Wells
Branch Line to Upwell
Branch Lines around Weymouth
Branch Lines around Wimborne
Branch Lines around Wisbech

NARROW GAUGE BRANCH LINES
Branch Line to Lynton
Branch Lines around Portmadoc 1923-46
Branch Lines around Porthmadog 1954-94
Branch Line to Southwold
Two-Foot Gauge Survivors

SOUTH COAST RAILWAYS
Ashford to Dover
Brighton to Eastbourne
Chichester to Portsmouth
Dover to Ramsgate
Hastings to Ashford
Portsmouth to Southampton
Ryde to Ventnor
Worthing to Chichester

SOUTHERN MAIN LINES
Bromley South to Rochester
Charing Cross to Orpington
Crawley to Littlehampton
Dartford to Sittingbourne
East Croydon to Three Bridges
Epsom to Horsham
Exeter to Barnstaple
Exeter to Tavistock
Faversham to Dover
Haywards Heath to Seaford
London Bridge to East Croydon
Orpington to Tonbridge
Swanley to Ashford
Tavistock to Plymouth
Victoria to East Croydon

Waterloo to Windsor
Waterloo to Woking
Woking to Portsmouth
Woking to Southampton
Yeovil to Exeter

EASTERN MAIN LINES
Fenchurch Street to Barking

COUNTRY RAILWAY ROUTES
Andover to Southampton
Bournemouth to Evercreech Jn.
Burnham to Evercreech Junction
Croydon to East Grinstead
Didcot to Winchester
Fareham to Salisbury
Frome to Bristol
Guildford to Redhill
Porthmadog to Blaenau
Reading to Basingstoke
Reading to Guildford
Redhill to Ashford
Salisbury to Westbury
Strood to Paddock Wood
Taunton to Barnstaple
Wenford Bridge to Fowey
Westbury to Bath
Woking to Alton
Yeovil to Dorchester

GREAT RAILWAY ERAS
Ashford from Steam to Eurostar
Clapham Junction 50 years of change
Festiniog in the Fifties
Festiniog in the Sixties
Isle of Wight Lines 50 years of change
Railways to Victory 1944-46

LONDON SUBURBAN RAILWAYS
Caterham and Tattenham Corner
Charing Cross to Dartford
Clapham Jn. to Beckenham Jn.
Crystal Palace and Catford Loop
East London Line
Finsbury Park to Alexandra Palace
Holborn Viaduct to Lewisham
Kingston and Hounslow Loops
Lewisham to Dartford
Lines around Wimbledon
London Bridge to Addiscombe
North London Line
South London Line
West Croydon to Epsom
West London Line
Willesden Junction to Richmond
Wimbledon to Epsom

STEAM PHOTOGRAPHERS
O.J.Morris's Southern Railways 1919-59

STEAMING THROUGH
Steaming through Cornwall
Steaming through East Sussex
Steaming through the Isle of Wight
Steaming through Kent
Steaming through West Hants
Steaming through West Sussex

TRAMWAY CLASSICS
Aldgate & Stepney Tramways
Barnet & Finchley Tramways

Bath Tramways
Bournemouth & Poole Tramways
Brighton's Tramways
Bristol's Tramways
Camberwell & W.Norwood Tramways
Clapham & Streatham Tramways
Dover's Tramways
East Ham & West Ham Tramways
Edgware and Willesden Tramways
Eltham & Woolwich Tramways
Embankment & Waterloo Tramways
Enfield & Wood Green Tramways
Exeter & Taunton Tramways
Gosport & Horndean Tramways
Greenwich & Dartford Tramways
Hampstead & Highgate Tramways
Hastings Tramways
Holborn & Finsbury Tramways
Ilford & Barking Tramways
Kingston & Wimbledon Tramways
Lewisham & Catford Tramways
Liverpool Tramways 1. Eastern Routes
Liverpool Tramways 2. Southern Routes
Maidstone & Chatham Tramways
North Kent Tramways
Portsmouth's Tramways
Reading Tramways
Seaton & Eastbourne Tramways
Southampton Tramways
Southend-on-sea Tramways
Southwark & Deptford Tramways
Stamford Hill Tramways
Thanet's Tramways
Victoria & Lambeth Tramways
Waltham Cross & Edmonton Tramways
Walthamstow & Leyton Tramways
Wandsworth & Battersea Tramways

TROLLEYBUS CLASSICS
Croydon Trolleybuses
Bournemouth Trolleybuses
Maidstone Trolleybuses
Reading Trolleybuses
Woolwich & Dartford Trolleybuses

WATERWAY ALBUMS
Kent and East Sussex Waterways
London's Lost Route to the Sea
London to Portsmouth Waterway
Surrey Waterways
West Sussex Waterways

MILITARY BOOKS
Battle over Sussex 1940
Blitz over Sussex 1941-42
Bombers over Sussex 1943-45
Bognor at War
Military Defence of West Sussex
Secret Sussex Resistance

OTHER BOOKS
Betwixt Petersfield & Midhurst
Brickmaking in Sussex
Changing Midhurst
Garraway Father & Son
Index to all Stations
South Eastern & Chatham Railways
London Chatham & Dover Railway

SOUTHERN RAILWAY VIDEO
War on the Line